Boardcraft:
Building Corporate Board Intelligence

By:

Devin A. Jopp, Ed.D.

Copyright © 2016 by Devin A. Jopp, Ed.D.

All rights reserved.

No part of this book may be reproduced or transmitted for resale or use by any party other than the individual purchaser who is the sole authorized user of this information. Purchaser is authorized to use any of the information in this publication for his or her own use only. All other reproduction or transmission, or any form or by any means, electronic or mechanical, including photocopying, recording or by any informational storage or retrieval system, is prohibited without express written permission from the author.

Devin A. Jopp, Ed.D.

Introduction

Over the past 20 years of my career, I've noticed that one of the most arcane and misunderstood structure of an organization is the board of directors. Through my experience as staff, CEO, COO and as a board director, I've observed that while boards tend to think of themselves as unique, they are far more similar to each other. The challenges that they face tend to fall in several common categories.

These common categories of problems I have identified as elements of "Corporate Board Intelligence (CB-IQ)". Boards tend to take on a life of themselves, beyond the individual members. As humans have intelligence, so too do corporate boards. Some boards work to advance their collective intelligence and build board capabilities while others quietly erode the organizations they serve through inaction or negligence

This book is part a fictional story and also a very real instruction manual. Its first part consists of a story about Coppryx, a fictional organization that struggles with an emerging competitor and stagnation at the board level. The second part of the book is a reference guide for boards of director and is intended to provide the reader with an overview of the elements of CB-IQ, how to assess their current state, and what boards can do to improve their CB-IQ.

Start at the Start

It just seemed like yesterday when Tina and Kevin would meet over coffee to talk about the dreams of building Coppryx, a firm specialized in selling medical devices to hospitals.

Back then, Tina, a long-time friend, served as an informal advisor to Kevin and helped mentor Kevin, who admittedly, loved innovation but was not very adept leader of people.

In the early days, Kevin was able to keep his hand on almost every detail until their business skyrocketed with a government contract and two acquisitions. The organization quickly outpaced Kevin's ability to manage by himself and over time hired a management team of 5 vice presidents underneath him.

In the beginning, Kevin asked Tina to help form the first informal advisory board, made up of 3 individuals with whom Tina had previously known quite well and had mutual respect with over the years. Both she and VJ Singh remained when the advisory board was replaced with a formal board of directors a year later.

But that was then, and this is now.

Coppryx had now managed to grow from 5 employees initially, to over one hundred as they watched their profits soar to over $150 million in the past 12 months. Two years ago Kevin, in consultation with Tina and the advisory board decided to take the company public. Going public definitely seemed to be the right thing to do but the organization and the board now just seemed so bureaucratic.

When the company went public, the advisory board was abolished and replaced with a formal governing board of directors consisting of 10 members. At the time, it was thought the expansion of the board would help grow the company's influence, open up greater sales and grant the organization access to other skills that it currently didn't have on the staff.

Tina agreed to serve as the first chair of the board. By all accounts, Tina's tenure as chair had been a "cake-walk" as the organization flourished. However, tensions around recruiting had dogged Tina for years, but with time she found it easier to avoid dealing with the issue. Her adage was, "why fix it if it isn't broken". Tina's tenure is coming to an end and it was not yet clear who her successor would be. She feels relieved to be near the finish line and hopes to not rock the boat before her term ends.

Cast of Characters

Tina Hernandez

Tina just turned 72 and was a longstanding member of the board since the early days of the company when the informal advisory board was put in place. Tina always remembered the day when she and Kevin first chatted about the big dreams of Coppryx becoming a true innovative force in providing medical devices to the healthcare market.

Tina was highly regarded and respected on the board, having previously served as a successful chief operating officer for a large software firm and was very well liked by other board directors. Tina had taken over as chair four years ago after the prior chair could no longer serve out his term due to suffering a debilitating car accident. Tina's term is set to expire soon but unfortunately there is no clear successor.

Kevin Morehouse

Kevin, age 52, was a technology entrepreneur through and through. He loved the thrill of the chase but detested anything that smelled of bureaucracy. At 6'5 feet tall, Kevin towered over most everyone he met. He started off his professional career as an engineer and managed to build the first medical devices for Coppryx in his home basement. Kevin loved his role as an entrepreneur and always felt more comfortable in managing the engineering department. He always considered himself a "techie" and had no patience at all for organizational politics.

Melanie Netfrit

Melanie, aged 46, was a younger board member and ran her own technology staffing firm. To meet Melanie was an understatement. She commanded respect when she entered a room, an extraordinarily bright, well-spoken and well-presented woman. When Melanie spoke, people listened as she had an amazing level of confidence and influence.

As a board director, Melanie ran hot and cold. She would always come for meetings, but would later be absent between gatherings and would tend to not participate in other activities outside of the formal board meetings. However, Melanie had managed to leverage her seat on the board by making new connections with other firms that had been great referral sources back to her own staffing firm. She was always nervous about losing her seat and saw it as a crucial source for new clients for her business. Melanie was also elected as the corporate secretary for the board.

Jerry Rooper

Jerry, age 58, was Tina's same age and was an early founding board member who first joined the board eight years ago. Jerry was a rather portly fellow whose appearance could be described as slightly unkempt.

Occasionally, over drinks Jerry would brag about this as his management style in his own organization where he served as a divisional vice director. "I bust my folk's chops and question people to get the most out of them," Jerry once bragged. However, to most board directors, Jerry was just plain painful. Jerry had a bad habit of turning questions into long-drawn-out opinions and endless comments.

Jerry served as the board treasurer, a role he thoroughly enjoyed as it allowed him to roll in the details of finance. Jerry prided himself as the voice of skepticism on the board and took it as his role to regularly ask the difficult and uncomfortable questions that no one else wanted to ask.

VJ Singh

Kevin and VJ were old college roommates back in the 80s when they were both completing their computer science programs at George Washington University. VJ just turned 60 this year and was quite a distinguished looking man with a silver mane of hair, always dressed in a fine suit. He had a very successful career in retail sales and retired several years ago after cashing in his stock options.

Early on, when Coppryx was just a concept, VJ became an early investor and served as the first member of the informal advisory board almost 10 years ago. When VJ retired, he kept his seat on the Coppryx board and at the same remained fully committed to growing the organization. However, he had concerns over the past several years around the lack of new candidates being considered for the board of directors. VJ agreed to serve as the chair of the nominating committee this year.

Ron James

Ron is the newest kid on the block. A young upstart, he just celebrated his 34th birthday and could best be described as a whiz-kid. Ron was no stranger to boards of directors, having served on several boards for local nonprofit charities and one small entrepreneurial board focused on developing security devices in the Washington DC's tech corridor.

Ron himself served as a CEO of a small technology services firm that provided guidance to the investment community. This past year, Ron won the "40 Under 40 Award" presented by the local Chamber of Commerce and was the epitome of the young tech entrepreneur. It was not uncommon to see Ron coming into the office in blue jeans, a polo shirt and flip flops when the weather was right (or wrong for that matter).

Paul Klammer

Paul, age 78, was one of the oldest members of the board and was just returning back to the board of directors after taking off some time due to an illness. After he had sold his firm several years earlier, he decided to move out of the DC area down to Amelia Island in Florida. Paul could best be described as the perfect combination of business casual meets island casual, with a button down patterned shirt and gray dress slacks. Paul's reputation over the years was of a soft-spoken person but one who carried a big stick as well. However, his illness set him back from being able to be more active and engaged in the daily affairs at Coppryx over the past several years.

Rachel Kim, Tim Stevens, Michael Owens

Rachel, Tim and Michael all served on the board of directors for Coppryx but rarely participated in the activities of the board. Each of them held relatively mid-level positions within larger firms in the healthcare sector and consequently found it difficult to juggle their careers with the responsibilities of being a board director at the same time.

Jimmy Rollins

Jimmy Rollins joined as the Chief Financial Officer for Coppryx about 2 years ago. Jimmy had earned his CPA the year prior and had just turned 27. He was an incredible professional and had brilliant skills, but was extremely socially complex. Jimmy was truly a wizard when it came to finances, but not a great collaborator. He genuinely enjoyed his work but didn't want to be bothered with other details he did not have the full control over (especially marketing).

Vanessa Higgins

Vanessa Higgins joined as the Vice President of Business Development around the same time as Jimmy did as CFO. Vanessa was extremely skilled and adept at marketing and sales. She truly loved developing social and business contacts and loved the thrill of sales even more. She led the marketing department to double digit growth for each of the past ten years.

Vanessa loved to close a particular deal but was terrible and really struggled at planning or managing details around the sales process. Kevin complained over her last two performance evaluations that while she could close the sales, actually he never felt that he had adequate insights into how her shop operated. However, he couldn't argue with her positive results as Coppryx continued to steadily grow year over year.

Devin A. Jopp, Ed.D.

Table of Contents

Introduction 3
Start at the Start 5
Cast of Characters 7

Chapter 1: Another Board Meeting 17
    Entanglement 22
    Readying the Pitch 24
    Nothing Beats Mondays 26
    The Unexpected 32
    The Wind Up 36
    The Pitch 41
    The Model 46
        Innovation Deficiency 48
        Environmental Maladaptation 54
        Influence Impotence 59
        Recruiting Stagnation 66
        Network Misalignment 72
        Accountability Shortage 78
        Power Imbalance 84
        Wrap-Up 87

Chapter 2: Turning Point 91
    Explosions 94
    Environmentally Centered 98
    Change of Guard 103
    To Be or Not to Be 106

Chapter 3: Lasting Changes 111
    Board Structure Shake-Up 112
    Board Performance Evaluations 116

Deeper Controversy: Board Mentors 117
Onwards and Upwards 119
Take-Off 122
Brand New Day 124

Chapter 4: Corporate Board Intelligence (CB-IQ) 127
Assessing CBIQ Vulnerabilities 131
Evaluating Scores 132
Element #1: Recruitment Stagnation 133
    Symptoms 134
    Prevention & Treatment Strategies 136
Element #2: Network Misalignment 148
    Symptoms 149
    Prevention & Treatment Strategies 151
Element #3: Power Imbalance 152
    Symptoms 153
    Prevention & Treatment Strategies 154
Element #4: Accountability Inadequacy 155
    Symptoms 156
    Prevention & Treatment Strategies 157
Element #5: Innovation Deficiency 159
    Symptoms 159
    Prevention & Treatment Strategies 161
Element #6: Environmental Maladaptation 162
    Symptoms 163
    Prevention & Treatment Strategies 164
Element #7: Influence Impotence 165
    Symptoms 166
    Prevention & Treatment Strategies 167
Where's Leadership 168

Summary 170
Dedication 171

Chapter 1:
Another Board Meeting

It was October and time for the last board meeting of the year for Coppryx. As the light broke through at the start of the day, the board of directors gathered in a conference room at hotel outside of Washington, DC. Kevin was feeling confident as ever, he had long held a great winning streak since the founding of Coppryx and this board meeting represented his 10th year in a row of double digit revenue growth.

Tina, who had served as chair for the past four years, would only be serving for 4 more months before her term would come to an end. Secretly, she was relieved to be at the end of her tenure with Coppryx. Being chair for the company wasn't really a hard job for her, it was mainly ceremonial at this point as she would preside over the compensation plan, the annual financial audit and the re-election process of the board of directors. Tina trusted

Kevin implicitly and would boast to fellow directors that "Coppryx was run on auto-pilot" practically.

However, Tina was always uncomfortable managing the strong personalities of the board and tried to avoid conflict whenever possible. She felt that the board tended to get mired in details that it probably didn't need to get involved with, but with the organization running smoothly, she once again preferred to avoid addressing such issues as it wasn't "broke".

One of the first agenda items for the fall board meeting was devoted to reviewing the company's strategic plan. Every year at this time, Tina would lead the board in reviewing the document. She referenced the strategic plan that had been included in the board packet, as the shuffle of page turning could be heard as all of the members turned to it in their board binders.

Tina knew that most, if not everyone had not read their packets, which was the norm at Coppryx, so she read the strategic plan headers off and the top three key strategies under each of the five focus areas. At the end, she asked: "Does anyone have any changes?"

Everyone just shook their head and within 30 minutes the strategic planning review was once again complete. Tina truly believed that the strategic plan was actually quite perfunctory at this point given the immense growth the organization had enjoyed. She whispered to Kevin: "Why mess with a winning formula?"

Another order of business for the day was the appointment of committee chairs as part of the annual fall board meeting ritual. There were only three standing committees of the board, including the executive, finance and audit committee, and nominating and governance committee. Each year the board would appoint committee chairs. As chair of the board, Tina would lead the executive committee along with Jerry as treasurer leading the finance and audit committee, and VJ would serve as the chair for the nominating and governance committee. Together, with Tina, they would form the executive committee of the larger board with Paul as an appointed ad hoc member of the executive committee.

As VJ heard his name called out as the new chair for the nominating and governance committee, he had a sinking feeling in his stomach. He knew that the board had a long standing problem of electing the same individuals and had a challenge in attracting new talent. He wasn't very excited about serving as chair of committee that acted like a "toothless dog," as VJ put it. Nonetheless, he did accept the position hoping to try to advance things a bit further over the next year, but in reality he didn't hold out hope for significant change at this point given the board's long-standing opposition to structural changes.

Tina yielded the floor over to VJ to provide his first nominating committee update. As VJ got up to present his report, he thought that this would look like the exact same speech he had heard at almost every board meeting for the past ten years, which included an overview of the recruiting process and a call to the board of directors to refer candidates for consideration.

In the midst of his report on the board activities, Jerry Rooper interrupted him: "VJ, you know our nominating process has been garbage for years, and yet here we are again talking about using the same process." VJ knew Jerry very well over the years and was fully aware that he was the type of character that tended to always attack things just to see how someone would react.

"Yes, I'm familiar with our challenge here, Jerry," VJ responded. "But short of us wholesale changing our recruiting process mid-stream, I don't see us making a change this year. What we can do now is start the discussion for next year."

Jerry shook his head in discontent. "VJ, that's a no-go. We need to do something different this year as the outcome always is the same." While Jerry was difficult at times, some would say all the time, he did have a point.

Before VJ could step back in to lob another volley, Tina stopped the feud: "Jerry, we have a lot of material to get through here today. Can we just table this till the February retreat?"

Jerry grudgingly accepted as blood seemed to drain red into his face. Clearly he was disappointed that the board would not take immediate action to fix the process.

VJ, noting the tension in the air, decided to take a consensus approach and suggested: "Perhaps the nominating committee could look at what options we could take on and then report back at our board retreat, so we would not start from ground zero?"

Tina nodded in agreement and concurred with VJ to move forward, however, not before Jerry interrupted again and offered, "Just make sure I'm on that group, VJ. I have some ideas that I want to make sure they don't get wiped under the rug."

VJ resented the notion that he would ever do such a thing but begrudgingly wrote down Jerry's name. He thought to himself that Jerry always seemed to be injecting himself into processes in such a manner and while he makes grand statements, usually his participation would just slow things down.

Sitting next to VJ was Melanie Netfrit, who whispered to him: "That Jerry is such a pain in the ass, he's always talking over everyone and dragging out this meeting needlessly." VJ nodded in agreement.

He thought very highly of Melanie but knew she had a propensity to be catty and would take anything you said and later use it in conversations with other board members. VJ was always careful when talking to Melanie, even when agreeing with her. He recalled one time when he made a comment to her about concerns he had about a new product launch, which ended up getting back to the chair courtesy of Melanie. In that case, she had gone back to Tina after speaking with VJ and told her that he was leading resistance against the new product launch. Of course, she didn't bother mentioning the fact that she had previously told VJ she also felt the same way. After that experience, he avoided entanglements with Melanie the much he could.

The board meeting concluded after reviewing several other pieces of business and was set to convene again over winter in order to pick up their annual retreat.

Entanglement

With the conclusion of the meeting done, Melanie came over to VJ.

"I really want to be on that little group you're putting together," Melanie offered.

Reluctantly, VJ agreed to add Melanie to the group as he figured better to have her on the group rather than not.

"Thank you so much VJ for the hard work you're putting into the nominating committee. I'm really looking forward to helping out and identifying some concrete actions we can take," she said.

After VJ left the room, Melanie walked over to Jerry who was packing up his black leather suitcase. "Jerry, I really think you're onto something here. The whole nominating committee process is broken and I think VJ really needs our leadership to pull this off."

Jerry nodded in agreement and was always happy to have someone agree with him.

"Next week I'll give you a call, Jerry, right after I get back so that you and I can get on the same page before we get on the call with VJ."

Jerry agreed with her proposal and left quickly to catch his noon flight out of Washington-Dulles airport.

Melanie glanced over at Tina, who was finishing up some notes from the meeting, and said: "Tina, I know VJ is going to do a great job putting this team together, but I did want to make sure you knew that I really don't see what problem we are trying to fix here exactly. I know Jerry thinks it's broken, but I want to make sure that whatever we do, we don't make any changes that will impact the current directors; I've been on this board almost since the beginning and any kind of changes shouldn't impact those of us who have the most wisdom and tenure."

Tina listened intently to Melanie and replied: "Let's wait and see when the report comes back, but I hear what you're saying."

Having said that, Melanie walked out of the room with Tina still chatting about the weather and what their respective plans were for the long weekend ahead. As Tina came out of the board meeting, she ran into Kevin at the elevator.

"Kevin, Melanie isn't thrilled about what we're doing here on the nominating committee."

Kevin gave an understanding nod and responded: "If it follows the path these conversations always take, I'm not sure there is anything to worry about, Tina."

Kevin, for his part, really didn't feel strongly either way about it, but did have a feeling that there were more than a few members of the board of directors that didn't really contribute on a regular basis. He felt Melanie was one of those. He thought that she seemed to be present at the meetings but wasn't very involved between them, so he was a little bit suspicious about her desire to take part in this issue, assuming it was just a defense strategy.

"Yes, we'll see where this all goes but I do share your optimism," she smiled back at Kevin.

Readying the Pitch

With the board meeting behind them, the holiday season was quickly approaching and VJ wanted to schedule the nominating committee teleconference quickly so as to not lose momentum. As Melanie read the meeting invitation email, she was dialing Jerry to coordinate their messaging. "Jerry, this is Melanie, so great to chat with you. How is your family doing?"

Jerry proceeded to fill Melanie in over the phone on his recent divorce and all of the rest struggles in his personal life. It didn't take much for Jerry to want to talk about his woes and Melanie knew that it would make for a great icebreaker to serve as a therapist for a few minutes.

Finally, Melanie broke into the conversation: "We need to make sure that VJ receives some leadership from us on this issue of recruiting new board directors."

"You know, Melanie, we just need to blow up this whole recruiting process and start over. It's totally useless, it's a rubber stamped process," replied Jerry.

Melanie listened intently and knew that Jerry needed to get the "steam out of his engine". She swiveled in her leatherback executive chair and put her legs up on her glass desk. "Jerry, why don't we come up with a checklist of desired attributes and traits that we want for the new board of directors? Let's just start with that, at least as a down payment for future changes that we all agree need to be made."

"That's not good enough alone, Melanie," retorted Jerry back. "We need to get the folks that aren't doing anything off the board as soon as possible and make room for those that actually want to contribute".

Melanie thought about Jerry's point for a moment but was still concerned that any move to change the board's composition would mean she would lose her seat. "Think about it for a minute, Jerry", she responded. "I really believe we need to be more strategic here and try not to tick off the entire board by suggesting they all shouldn't have their seats. How about we consider doing something at the end of the terms of the board, since we are staggered?"

Melanie knew that she was just elected to a new three-year term, so she would be one of the last ones to be subjected to whatever new criteria would be developed. Besides, she considered if history was a predictor, she didn't believe at all that the issue was going anywhere.

After some further debate, Jerry agreed with Melanie's phased-in approach proposal that they push for a meaningful change in the recruiting process. With the call ended, the table was now set for the nominating committee's taskforce call the following Monday.

Nothing Beats Mondays

"Nothing like a nominating committee call first thing Monday morning", VJ thought to himself as he took a sip of coffee from his Washington Nationals mug. VJ felt a little bit apprehensive about the call as he himself had seen this same effort implode many times prior and didn't want to be the one to preside over the latest brawl.

Melanie, Jerry, and Tina joined the call first and later Tim joined them, which surprised about everyone given the usual lack of participation. Kevin also decided to hop on the call in order to keep tabs on the way the discussion proceeded.

VJ opened the meeting and welcomed the participants. First, he noted the long-standing challenge that the board severally faced in the past, namely how to structure it and the kind of candidates the board wanted for the upcoming year. VJ emphasized that the nominating committee's priority should be the immediate recruiting process for new candidates, noting that they traditionally put out a call for new nominations in early summer in order to be able to solicit interest. He also reminded them that the proper procedure should be kept, both the filled out questionnaire and candidate's current CV should be returned back. The nominating committee would then review the applicants and present them to the board for selection.

True to form, Jerry broke in over top of VJ: "I'm personally tired of members of the rubber stamping process we go through here to vet new candidates that just take up oxygen." Jerry continued his diatribe: "VJ, it's your turn at bat here to firmly make a stand and fix these problems. We need this nominating committee to make the hard decisions here on these candidates before they go to the board and make sure the basic criteria are met."

VJ gave Jerry a few minutes and tried to reign him in a bit, but it wasn't terribly effective. Finally, he caught a break: "Listen Jerry, I agree, but we need to step into this and design something everyone can live with."

VJ knew that Jerry was right but always got agitated when he went on the offensive, as he always tended to do. VJ tried to think about the best strategy to try to walk away with some sort of progress on this call, when Tina broke in: "Jerry, you act like we have a ton of board candidates beating our door down and that's just not the case."

VJ sat back and waited for the next volleys to come as Tina had just pitched a hand grenade into the conversation. Tim tried to say something but was suddenly cut off by Jerry, whose blood pressure could literally be felt through the phone.

"Tina, that's because we think that the right board candidates will just come to our door," replied Jerry, "Maybe that's why we have a 20/80 problem - 20% of the board does 80% of the work. Frankly, the boards I know do most of this through recruiting individuals they know personally and don't even play around with a call for nomination."

The lines in the sand were now clearly drawn and Melanie had waited for the dust to clear before wading into the fray, "I've been silently sitting here listening to the points being made and I think Jerry is really onto something here, but we need to be cautious not to implement change too quickly. I think for now, we should develop a criteria set of what we want out of the new board directors and send that out in our nominating process. That way, the individuals can see the requirements that we need before submitting their nominations. The nominating committee can then review the applicants to see if they fit the criteria set."

Silence filled the gap in the conversation for a moment, but not for long. Jerry couldn't be contained any further.

"If we want to just move the ball five yards down the field, we can do that, or we can just change this nominating process to make it meaningful," Jerry proposed.

VJ watched from the sidelines trying to figure out the best method to advance the conversation. Trying to move anything forward at this point via a teleconference call he thought would be rather impractical. VJ weighed in: "So, given the challenge with the board not being able to meet in person and the need to hit our annual recruiting timeframe, let's move forward with the changes."

"Maybe then we re-visit this at our next meeting in order to see if we can make more substantial changes for the next year," Melanie suggested.

VJ knew he was shutting down the discussion. He needed to get this call over within an hour and still had the hairy issue of board composition unaddressed. Everyone including Jerry fell silent. VJ was aware of the fact that he had just sucked the life out of the conversation but wanted to move ahead and try to salvage something from the call.

"We have a second issue that we need to discuss as well," continued VJ. "We need to figure out what the optimum board composition should look like. We all know that as the board has evolved, we don't get a lot of participation from folks on the board and many of those aren't business development types or hold rolodexes that could help Coppryx."

VJ didn't get through his last sentence without Melanie drowning out the end of his thoughts. Melanie thought about her discussion with Jerry but decided to make a calculated play to slow down the discussion: "VJ, I don't think changing the existing board is really an issue we can tackle today. We really should focus on the recruiting process for new board directors and leave this for some other time in the future."

Jerry was furious. He thought Melanie agreed on their pre-call to push for changes at the end of each term for board directors. "Melanie, that's totally wrong - we need to get some real workhorses on this board and come up with a plan on how to do it," Jerry responded.

"We have workhorses on this board, Jerry," Tina chimed in again, "and you're talking to them right now," she said with a chuckle.

Jerry wasn't amused at all and continued his frontal assault: "I think we need to scrap the existing board and just start over."

Kevin remained fairly quiet during the heated exchange trying to maintain objectivity in the discussion as the CEO, but he was pleased that Jerry was being unreasonable.

"I agree with you, Jerry," Melanie jumped in, "that there are things that we can do differently with our board appointments. I just think we have to pace ourselves and honor the great work we have done, before we throw it all away. How about we discuss this at the February board meeting? We could come up with a recommendation to make changes based on when the terms of board directors expire, so that it doesn't impact everyone at once."

Jerry was pleased to see Melanie back their earlier agreement and decided to not push the point given that their hour was up for the call.

VJ moved in quickly to wrap up the meeting, clearly exhausted but was somewhat content that there was at least some semblance of a path forward.

Immediately after the call-conference, he picked up the phone and contacted the CEO: "Kevin, I don't see any way that we're really going to get meaningful change to board composition next year. We're just going to have to try to chip away at this problem by raising the bar for new board members."

Kevin had been down this road many times and he agreed with VJ that the election process would remain largely the same. "How about you work up a strawman for the new desired traits of board directors,' Kevin replied back, "and later we can present a strawman to the board for them to review at the next meeting?"

VJ and Kevin would spend the next two months working on a sample board job description, which included desired traits and skills that they hoped would be approved at the next meeting.

The Unexpected

As the Christmas holiday approached, Kevin sat at his desk going over the latest quarterly financial reports that his CFO, Jimmy Rollins, had prepared for him.

"Jimmy, something is extremely wrong here," Kevin said with his face turning slightly red as he peered up at Jimmy who was standing next to his desk. "Do you have any idea why this is happening?" Kevin asked after regaining his composure.

"I can't be certain, as that's marketing function. The new sales revenue numbers are way off target, representing a drop of 35% compared to last year," Jimmy explained.

Kevin was now standing. "What! Do you mean you can't be certain, Jimmy? It's your job to be on top of these things," he said.

"I'm just the messenger and am telling you the numbers. I'm not your marketing vice president," Jimmy replied with a hint of sarcasm.

Kevin thought he sounded like the medical doctor (Bones) from Star Trek telling the captain that he was a doctor, not a bricklayer. Jimmy had a panache for being snarky, which Kevin chalked it up to a personality deficiency he earned by studying credits and debits for a living. However, at this moment, he literally wanted to wring his neck.

Soon enough, Kevin regained his composure and called on Vanessa to join them to discuss the variance further. Vanessa came into the office, lacking her normal sense of self-confidence.

"I'm sure you know why I asked you to join us," he said in an ominous tone.

"I just read the latest financials this morning," Vanessa responded.

"How come we didn't see this coming?" Kevin asked. "In just one quarter we managed to lose 35% of our sales volume and somehow I wasn't given any kind of warning about this."

Vanessa had never seen Kevin so angry, but she knew herself that she wasn't quite sure either why the numbers had plummeted so fast recently. But she had a clue of who they were losing ground to.

"This isn't just a sales problem, Kevin," Vanessa leveled with him. "I think there is a bigger problem with our technology. It is outdated and we can't convince the clients when they see NecroTech's product and ours side-by-side. Even the best sales people in the world can't sell a product if it's obviously inferior," Vanessa concluded.

Kevin was pretty sure that he was about to burst an artery and clutched the edge of his desk, leaving finger nail marks on the side of the dark mahogany surface. "Maybe the problem here is that you're not confident in our products, Vanessa?" Kevin retorted. Sure, he wasn't being fair to Vanessa, but his anger had overwhelmed him at this point.

"You need to get our sales team in gear, Vanessa. We have one quarter to get these numbers back in line before I report the numbers at the next board meeting."

Kevin was nervous about delivering bad news back to the board at this time and didn't want to alarm anyone yet, at least not until he was absolutely sure that there was a trend.

"And why don't we have any intelligence on our pipeline, Vanessa? Kevin continued impatiently. "It's like we're always flying blind around here. We've been lucky so far, but our luck has run out obviously. "Kevin brought the meeting to a close as Vanessa and Jimmy both slinked out of the room. The last thing he wanted to be is an alarmist, but at the same time he needed to give Tina a heads-up and penned a note to her and the executive officers about the "downturn in the fourth quarter financials".

Over the next week, through a number of meetings with various internal team members, Kevin started to piece together what was happening and learned that a new competitor, NecroTech, had entered the market a few months prior and was cannibalizing their new client prospects.

Kevin knew his competitor well. The current company's CEO worked as the director of product development for a number of years for Coppryx. Kevin never took

NecroTech seriously as he had thought that their market lead was insurmountable. But the numbers weren't lying, they were now hemorrhaging sales and sinking fast.

As Kevin sat on his sofa that evening, he cupped his hands together and placed his head in hands, wondering how in the world he could solve the problem. He needed to come up with a solution, and fast. He remembered how hard they all had worked in the beginning to launch the product and differentiate themselves early on. And now, everything he worked for was simply being taken away from him seemingly overnight.

Kevin poured a rather healthy glass of merlot as he paced the living room. He took a slow lingering sip and grabbed his cell phone off the coffee table next to him. It was time to call Tina: "Tina, we have a big problem on our hands." Kevin proceeded to fill Tina in on the dire situation and the "loss of traction in the marketplace" over the past quarter.

Tina fell silent on the line and finally responded, "So what do you think we should do to get things back on track, Kevin? And what do we tell the rest of the board?"

"We're working it out at the moment Tina," Kevin responded. "I just don't have answers yet. I will work with the staff to develop a comprehensive plan for the board's consideration, but for now, I think we should just tell the board what is happening and our intention to submit a plan."

Tina agreed and suggested that the executive committee convene in the short term to discuss the issue, and at same time the board meeting should be extended to a two-day event in order to make sure everyone understands what is going on."

After Kevin agreed with the suggestion, Tina promised to get the notice out before ending the call. She hung up the phone wondering what was going to happen now. All she wanted was a peaceful exit from the chair position and now is presiding over the decline of the organization. Tina knew the next meeting was going to be contentious, there was no escaping it. "It had been so easy to lead for the past several years," Tina thought to herself, but the real test for her leadership may very well lay ahead.

The Wind Up

The February board meeting was being held this year at the historical Willard Hotel in downtown DC. A beautiful old hotel that traced its roots back to 1818 and had hosted every president since the 14th president in 1853.

As Kevin walked in, he was struck how the rather sedate sandstone exterior of the hotel suddenly gave way to an incredibly ornate lobby with white and tan swirled marble columns, highly polished white and black checkered marble floors, and intricate inlaid tray ceilings.

Kevin, Jimmy and Vanessa were the first to arrive into the lobby and checked into the hotel.

"Jimmy, Vanessa, please make sure you get the backup together for our discussion tomorrow so we could discuss the marketing pipeline and financials around all of this," Kevin ordered.

Both nodded in agreement and took the elevators upstairs to their rooms to continue with their meeting preparation. Kevin quickly dropped his bag off in his room and came back down to meet with Tina and VJ for cocktails at the lobby.

As Kevin walked into the Round Robin bar, he was struck by just how unique this place actually was. The bar was relatively small, completely round in shape with the walls as dark as holly tree leaves with mahogany wood accents. The center of the room boasted a round mahogany bar with a black marble bar top and black leather stools. Small tables encircled the bar. Kevin grabbed one of the small side tables and pulled up an extra chair. Then, without hesitation he ordered his favorite drink - a gin gimlet with fresh squeezed lime juice.

VJ, Paul and Tina came into the bar shortly afterwards, greeted each other and ordered a round of cocktails. A few moments later, Ron came into the bar having just arrived and was going to order dinner for himself before being beckoned over by Tina to join them. After exchanging the usual pleasantries, Tina started in: "Boy, we do have our work cut out for us here, don't we, Kevin?"

Kevin proceeded to provide context for tomorrow's meeting and explained how their market share was evaporating seemingly overnight. Paul pressed him, "So? What's the play on this, Kevin? Do you have an idea of what to do here?"

Kevin nervously tapped his fingers on his knee as he took a sip from his cocktail and placed it back on the glass top. "I've wracked my brain on this for the past couple of weeks and as I see it, we have no other choice but to go back and redesign our medical devices from the ground floor up. I hate to admit it but we're just not competitive right now."

With a clear look of concern on his brow, VJ quizzed Kevin further: "Are you saying we need to go back and rewrite the systems or redesign the hardware units? Either way that's cost prohibitive."

"I'm not sure yet to what extent but we're going to have to make an investment to break the cycle here," Kevin responded. "I don't see how we can make a change without doing so."

Tina listened intently and knew the board would not react well to a proposal to invest millions of dollars into a ground up re-do and they certainly aren't going to approve it now. Especially given the fact there was no effort made to try to "pre-sell" such a concept before this board meeting.

"This may be a multi-step process, Kevin," she said, "as I don't think we have the votes to push this through tomorrow."

"We can't take a quarter to study this one, Tina," Kevin noted. "I think we really need to move ahead on this."

"I hate to ask this question," suddenly Paul broke into the conversation, "but do we even know why we are not being selected? Do we know what our customers really want from us?"

Ron had been sitting silently listening to the exchange, took a sip from his drink and finally spoke up: "I think this is a lack of CBIQ."

A noticeable pause in the conversation filled the air. Tina took the bait first.

"Alright Ron, what in the hell are you talking about?" she asked with a smile.

"While we all tend to believe that each board is unique, and they are to some extent, there are many things that are pretty similar across every board of directors," Ron replied. "I remember learning many years ago about how people have emotional and social intelligence when dealing with their own emotions, social engagement and decision making. Actually, boards have the same issue but some differences since we function as a group. The ability of boards to understand their environments and to adapt to them is corporate board intelligence or corporate board IQ.

"Great, you're giving us an IQ test?" Paul erupted with a huge grin on his face.

"Not quite, Paul," Ron laughed. "I'm rather talking about challenges that boards make which have significant impact on the function of the organization for which they are charged with leading. For example, over drinks here we are talking about our competitor eating into our market share, but the fact that there is a new competitor on the scene isn't really our key problem, is it?"

"Maybe not," Tina responded.

"I think it's our biggest problem," Kevin laughed.

Paul broke up the silence and offered another wisecrack: "So, do you mean we are low IQ?"

"Sort of, Paul," Ron smiled, "but we need to face up to the things that we haven't done right in the past, and then correct them. That's the hard part - understanding what's really wrong and then finding a way to fix it. These sins tend to infest the souls of boards and eat them from the inside out. As a board, usually we are inclined to focus on the symptoms and not deal with the root cause."

Sensing where this was going, Kevin spoke up: "So what are you suggesting, Ron?"

"I'm suggesting that if all we do at this board meeting is to wring our hands about NecroTech and talk about our sales strategy at the next board meeting, in reality we will not be helping you to solve anything at all, Kevin."

Kevin sat silently, not really sure if he agreed with where Ron was heading with all of this.

"Ron, I'm not sure I'm with you on this," Paul broke in. "We're going to talk about everything except our sales strategy?"

"I think the sales strategy falls out of this, Paul," Ron followed up. "But if my hunch is right, we are going to find out that there are several things contributing to our most recent decline in sales."

Tina sat silent and agreed with Paul. She didn't really know where Ron was heading trying to make his point, but also thought they needed a framework to guide the discussion for the board meeting the next day, otherwise there was a real risk the meeting turning into a free-for-all.

Tina finished munching on the last handful of bar nuts and said: "Alright, Ron, we'll give you the ball to take down the field."

With that, the evening concluded and everyone retired for the evening in advance of the next day's meeting.

The Pitch

The next morning all members of the board convened in the conference room located on the first floor of the hotel. The room was cavernous for such a small group, but a large U-shaped table filled the middle of the room.

Before the room, Ron walked over to Tina and said: "Tina, I'd like to ask if you would mind moving the committee reports to the end of the meeting."

"Why?" Tina asked.

"I want to save our horsepower for "corporate board IQ" rather than listening to board reports first", he smiled.

Tina was skeptical about the need to change up the agenda but agreed with Ron's request. And so the day began with the board of directors milling in close to the eight o'clock witching hour. As everyone arrived, they exchanged greetings as they grabbed cups of coffee and took their time to set up their laptops.

As everyone took their seats, Tina opened the meeting. She dispensed with the normal pleasantries and set the tone right from the start: "I wish I had better news for everyone but as you have heard, we suffered a pretty big financial blow this past quarter with the entrance of a new competitor and the significant decline in our sales. I've decided to dispense with all non-essential reports and will be moving all committee reports to the end of this meeting."

Jerry cocked his head to the side and gave Tina a questioning look, but decided to leave it alone for now.

Kevin then took over and set the stage for the conversation: "As you all know, we've had an incredible journey here over the past ten years. But now we have a real crisis on our hands with a sales slump of 35% in the last quarter and our pipeline of prospective sales targets falling off at an alarming rate. We initially thought that perhaps it was a holiday slump, but the drop off is too steep. At this rate we will dip into our reserves within the next quarter at our existing staffing levels. Subsequently we would be out of reserves within two years at the current burn rate."

Silence fell over the board and a sense of panic was evident from the look on several of the directors' faces, as Kevin completed his background presentation showing a series of PowerPoint charts that painted the grim picture. Of course, everyone knew from the board materials and the grapevine that Coppryx had problems, but they had no idea just how bad it was.

Tina opened up the floor for questions for Kevin. However, instead of questions, a series of board directors fired off their comments and concerns.

"The real problem here," Paul led the charge, "is that we rested on our laurels over the past ten years and didn't invest enough back into our product. We're paying the piper on this and it's going to take real work for us to get back on track."

"Well Paul, it's a day late and a dollar short to start worrying about that now. Look, we built up a great reserve over the years so we can weather this storm."

Paul didn't buy into the argument that the healthy reserve was worth the current problem that they were facing. However, before he could respond, Melanie pressed forward: "How do we know this all isn't just a seasonal thing that we can outlive? Maybe we need to watch this for a while rather than jumping headfirst and squandering our savings."

"Melanie makes a really good point here," Rachel spoke up in support of her position. "Maybe this is just seasonal."

"I don't think seasonality explains a 35% drop-off really," VJ weighed in. "There's something amiss here."

"Listen folks, we don't have a full answer here yet, Kevin tried to wrest control of the discussion. "Taking potshots isn't going to get us anywhere."

However, the potshots continued until Tina intervened: "We need a path forward for our meeting. Before the meeting Ron approached me about how to frame the discussion and how we can set up our approach to solve this and some other challenges that we are facing. I'd like for us to try it out." With that, Tina turned the floor over to Ron.

He gave her a nod of appreciation, stood up and walked up to the front of the table with a large whiteboard and four flipcharts.

"Several years ago," Ron started, "I attended a seminar and learned about the "corporate board IQ" that explained how "smart' board think and process their challenges and identify solution. This concept helped to explain many of the challenges I encountered with various boards I served on and enabled me to make sense of the problems and how to solve them. The reality of being in any organization is that it's quite easy to get lost in the trees and to lose sight of the forest. I think that's what's happening to us right now. Even just being here for a relatively short time, I've already seen a number of signs that have concerned me about the future of this organization."

A nervous look fell over several of the directors who felt like the "new guy" was taking potshots. Ron felt the nervousness and pressed ahead: "What I'm going to explain to you is not easy to hear, I know. It will make us extremely uncomfortable. But if we want to be thriving ten years from now, we're going to need to ask those hard questions. The sales slump is terrible but it is only the tip of the iceberg. We have to make sure that we are addressing real root causes and not just symptoms".

Ron continued. "Like children that grow into adolescents and adults, so, too are boards. They develop and change over time. Problems that we encounter at one time, like learning to walk, we solve easily, and yet others are newer later on in life, like paying off a mortgage. My point is that boards also face different challenges in their development. How we equip ourselves as a board to address our environment and our challenges has to do with the level of corporate board intelligence that we have built. When we operate out of a high IQ, great things can happen for boards. However, if we are operating at a low IQ, then we can destroy the very boards we serve on and their organizational performance."

Ron made a short pause and Melanie immediately took the opportunity to challenge him: "So why do we need to know about "corporate board IQ" right now, when we really need to fix this problem with our sales slump?"

"If we only talked about the sales slump," Ron responded, 'there's a good chance we are going to miss what is causing the slump and get too single-focused on solving a symptom rather than the actual cause. Also bear in mind, some problems are so intertwined that you cannot fix one without addressing another first. We have to be willing to peel back the onion and look beneath."

Jerry hated cliffhangers and broke in: "Alright, Ron, enough stalling. Let's stop talking about onions and start talking about what are these seven sins."

"Great! You hung in there with me, Jerry," Ron smiled. "Let's dive in and start at the beginning."

The Model

Ron walked up to the whiteboard in the front of the room, grabbed a marker and drew a diagram of seven empty bubbles with a square on top called "Board Success".

"Every board has certain pieces that have to run well for it to be successful and ultimately for an organization to be successful," Ron began his lecture. "If one of those pieces doesn't work right, it can slow down the performance of the board or even bring it to a screeching halt. Imagine if board success rode on bed of two balls that all rolled together to propel it forward. What would happen if one of those balls fell out?"

"The whole thing would fall apart," Melanie responded, already looking bored.

Ignoring the tinge of sarcasm in her voice, Ron continued: "Right, it would definitely fall apart. So, our job here is to make sure that all of the parts work well together in order to ever avoid that from happening. In fact, one of the most important roles that we have as a board is to make sure we are the conductor for the great orchestra that must be in harmony for all of these things to work well. Normally, I might start at the bottom and work our way up," Ron continued after a short pause, "but given our unique situation with declining sales, I'm going to start here on one of the top bubbles first."

Innovation Deficiency

Ron filled in the first center bubble and noted: "Innovation deficiency is the first element of the seven that boards tend to encounter. When we say this, we mean specifically the tendency to suck your own exhaust pipe. This happens when boards and the organizations that serve them tend to not examine thoroughly what is really working and do not take on efforts to improve operations or market position. You see this often when boards tend to hold onto strategic plans that have far outlived their usefulness."

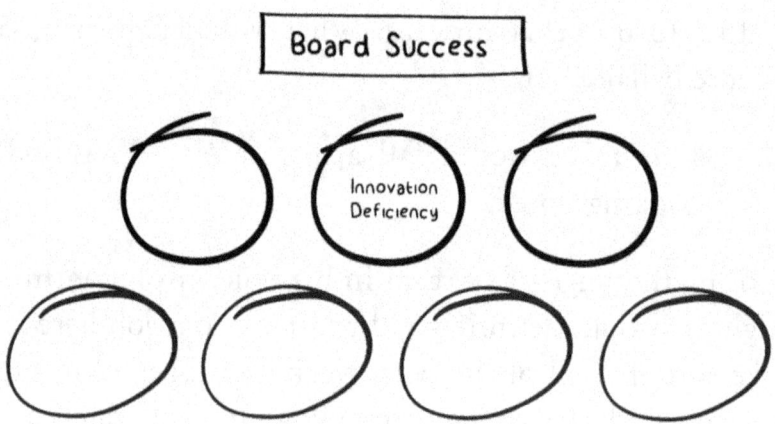

Paul had thought for quite some time that Coppryx never really invested enough money into research and development, and pounced on the idea: "Well, you hit the nail on the head on that one, Ron. Look at how we conducted our own strategic planning process earlier this year. We practically just rubber-stamped the damn thing and all of a sudden we're getting beaten to pieces."

Tina twitched in her seat, feeling that Paul was mounting an attack against her leadership and retorted: "All of this crap happened after our annual strategic reviewing process, so I really don't see how you are linking the two together."

Melanie grabbed the moment of silence and said: "Well, I don't think we have an innovation problem at all. I just think there is a seasonal slowdown and we're over-reacting a bit."

"I agree," Rachel latched onto the opportunity to support Melanie again. "I'm still not convinced that we have seen enough proof to know this isn't seasonal."

Ron felt like he was losing control of the conversation, but knew that there were some things below the surface that needed to come forward.

"Listen, we had a good thing going here and we got a lot of mileage out of our initial R&D efforts and strategic plan," VJ chimed in, "but we have a big sign being waved in our face right now that we need a change."

Jerry was unusually quiet but jumped in: "Well VJ, how the hell are we going to do this? There is no one on the board that knows the first thing about our marketplace or what kind of products and services they need."

An awkward silence filled the air. Ron seized the moment to push forward: "And we wouldn't be the first group, Jerry, that wouldn't have that expertise here. In fact, the thing about innovation is that you cannot plan it at all. If we were planting a field of wheat, could we control how every stalk of wheat will grow, how tall it will grow or how much wheat it would yield from one stalk? The only thing we can do is provide the right conditions for this to happen."

"What do you mean, Ron?" Kevin looked at Ron curiously.

"Innovation happens when we least expect it and sometimes in the most unplanned ways," Ron replied. "As a board, we need to create opportunities for spontaneous innovation to occur. Innovation works outside of a process, it doesn't follow our rules of timing and it is not predictable. So we can create the conditions for innovation to happen, but we cannot will it into existence."

"I got what you're saying, Ron," VJ followed. "I guess the more we try to structure things, ironically the more we may actually stifle innovation."

Usually quiet, Michael finally spoke up: "So, as a board, our role is to focus on making sure that the conditions are right for innovation to happen?"

Ron nodded and was glad to see folks were catching up but decided to push the point forward: "Exactly, Michael!

Companies go about different ways trying to be innovative. In some cases, they may try to buy innovation through acquisitions, and in most cases they try to self-generate new ideas. Think about companies that developed innovative ideas that changed our lives - for example smartphones, social media, the Internet, flat screen TVs etc. What's in common for these products is that they were all developed through a combination of conscious cultivation and a lot of luck. As a board, our job is to not only help provide Kevin what he needs to build an innovative organization through things like budget for experimentation (R&D), but we also need to create new ways that we can become more innovative as well. It's our responsibility to be an 'innovative' board."

"What exactly do you mean by that, Ron?" VJ interrupted with an unadulterated surprise written all over his face. "I don't really get what all this means in terms of actions."

"It simply means we need to take time at the board meetings to help plow the organization's fields," Ron happily responded. "There are many ways we can do this. In fact, let's break into teams and come up with some separate ideas about how we could encourage innovation as a board."

Ron broke the board up into 3 teams and appointed a team captain from each group to capture "wild and crazy" ideas that Coppryx could implement in order to open the board to innovation.

After a short pause, Ron brought the team back together and compiled the ideas.

"I love this one!" VJ said as he pointed to one of the ideas his group reported out – "invite outsiders to join board meeting on special deep-dive discussions".

Ron gathered the rest of the ideas from the breakout and highlighted a few of them:

1) Create special teams of board directors and outside folks to explore topics;
2) Create cross-industry board director swaps;
3) Make time to brainstorm instead of listening to reports;
4) Drill down sessions on top issues to explore improvement;

Ron finished writing on the whiteboard and Paul weighed in: "So you're saying we can stop sucking our own exhaust pipe if we do a few of these things?"

"Exactly, Paul," Ron smiled.

"Easier said than done, Ron," Melanie pounced. "We are not going to be able to make the switch easily, I just don't see it happening right away."

Ron contained his frustration around Melanie's attack: "I didn't say it was going to be easy. However, our role as the board is to not only keep the organization balanced but also be able to operate in a state of unbalance. If we want the organization that we govern to be innovative, we, the board members have to be innovative too."

He went over to one of the flip charts and drew a series of arrows.

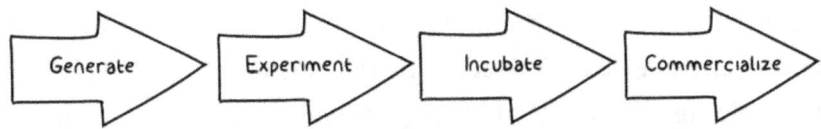

"When we think about innovation," continued Ron, "we're not just talking about the generation of new ideas, which should not be ignored by any means, but we also need to talk about innovation experimentation, incubation and commercialization. As a board, we have to help create the appropriate conditions by which we foster a healthy environment for innovation to be tested in, to fail, to nurture those viable ideas. Then we build an adequate structure to take those innovations to market in order to allow them to ultimately be monetized."

Tina had a light bulb moment: "Ron, I think I get what you're saying here. I guess you mean that we need to really think about how to create a pipeline for new ideas that ultimately expand our business."

"I have to admit, I'm an engineer but I never really thought about the board's role as spurring innovation," Kevin followed.

"Yes, that's why it's one of the elements of corporate board IQ," Ron answered. "Usually we tend to think about good governance in terms of audit reports, compensation task forces or board reports, but in reality the board itself needs to be an innovation catalyst."

Sensing the momentum from the morning session, Ron suggested to Tina that the board should take a break.

During the pause, Ron walked over to Kevin and Tina who were speaking to each other. Tina started in: "I was just telling Kevin that I think we should put a board taskforce on this and figure out how we can take this concept and make it actionable."

Tina's desire to move to a conclusion was obvious.

"Let's hang tight, Tina," Ron suggested, "till we get through all seven elements. I hate to say this, but board taskforces are often times places where good ideas go to get killed."

Kevin smiled, while a look of disbelief crossed Tina's face.

"I have one more board meeting left in me, Ron, so go for it," she said with a smile.

Michael approached Ron over the break and while normally relatively non-participatory, he expressed enthusiasm around the discussion on innovation. Ron was encouraged to see the message was starting to get through.

Environmental Maladaptation

When the board reconvened, Ron was busy filling in the second bubble.

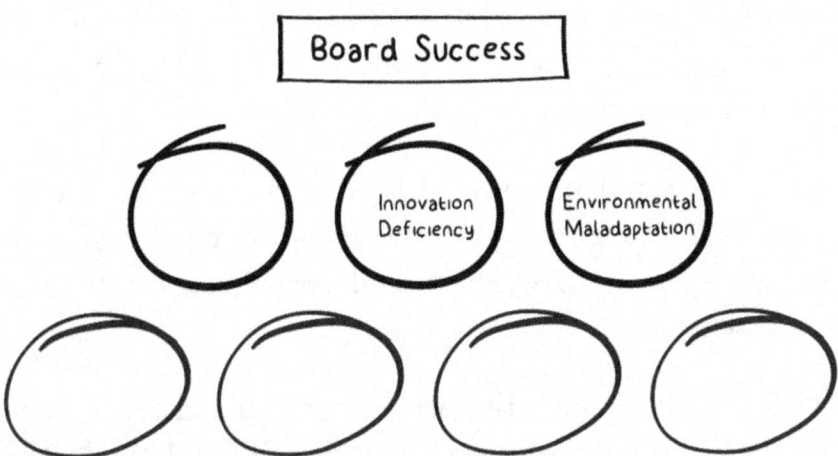

He kicked things off since everyone had their coffee fix over the break.

"Innovation deficiency was the first element of corporate board IQ," Ron continued, "but it's closely related to our second element- environmental maladaptation. When we say 'environmental maladaptation', we mean that something that seemed reasonable at some time has become less and less suitable, or has become a problem as time goes on. It's not to say that we were wrong from the beginning, rather the thing that we thought was right at the time, has become wrong."

"Sounds a lot like our products these days," VJ weighed in sarcastically. An audible chuckle came from the board.

"Listen, the world is full of things that were right at one time and are no longer right," Ron responded. "Think the Polaroid when the digital camera came out, or the poor buggy manufacturer when the car was invented. What about all the candle stick makers that were out of work when the light bulb came along? Now those are dramatic somewhat examples, but..."

Before he could finish, Paul jumped in: "But that's where we are. We have the horse and buggy medical device and our competitors have the brand new Porsche rolling off the assembly line."

Melanie was clicking the pen in her hand, clearly agitated by Paul's "shoot from the hip style". "Paul, I think that's ridiculous. I believe Kevin and the staff have done a great job over the years, and equating Coppryx to a 'horse' and 'buggy' is just asinine."

Of course, calling Paul anything close to an "ass" was enough to send him over the edge.

"Melanie, you can put your head in the sand all you want but we need to make some serious changes here," Paul retorted. "We need to pivot our direction and to implement some of these innovation changes that Ron laid out for us, otherwise we're going to be yesterday's news. You can attack me all you want, but it doesn't change the fact that we have serious work to do."

Tina was nervous about the exchange and leaned over to Kevin: "What do you make of this, Kevin?"

Kevin leaned in. "I think Paul's right here, Tina," he replied. "I'm not making these numbers up and if we pretend like they are not real, that's not going to help us at all."

Jerry cut in behind Paul: "And exactly how are we going to get all of this money in order to reinvent our products and services?"

"Okay, we're moving back into solutions instead of focusing on the seven elements of corporate board IQ," Ron jumped in front of the question. "We will get to a plan of action but let's stay here for a moment, please! The main issue here is that boards at times fall out of touch with their environments and stick with existing strategies even though market conditions have changed. Boards then fall prey to not adjusting appropriately to the market by not willing to assume enough risk to make the necessary adjustments to maintain market leadership, which consequently leads to stagnation. Sometimes board may take on too much risk, which can deplete the organization of resources."

"That's what I'm saying," Jerry once again broke in over Ron.

He ignored Jerry's latest barrage and continued: "However, boards of directors tend to error on the 'too little risk' and 'too little change'. It is the case of a day late and a dollar short. Once the board suffers from maladaptation, it is a difficult place to be because it requires them to have to get back in touch with the environment. It is a painfully difficult process because the board of directors will tend to hear things that may challenge what they have come to believe. And let's face it, at most board meetings we avoid confrontation and instinctively strive towards agreement.

Fighting that urge is difficult but necessary to overcome it."

VJ had been watching from the sidelines but finally joined in: "Sounds to me like it's time for us to get a little uncomfortable. So let me ask a question here. Do we even know why our competitor is gaining market share?"

"We think it's because our technology is older," Kevin replied.

VJ was not convinced by the CEO's answer and pressed Kevin harder: "Really? We know that for a fact? Have we actually spoken to our customers about this? Maybe we could think about a focus group with our customers and some board directors together to explore this and come up with some further intelligence here?"

Ron loved the energy and grabbed the moment. "Right, so what you're saying VJ is that maybe we lost touch with our client's needs. Let's capture this in the solutions parking lot", Ron said as he energetically jotted the idea on one of the flip charts.

"I'm just wondering how much this is going to cost us," Jerry added anxiously.

"It doesn't really matter, Jerry," Paul responded. "What's important is that we need to not sit on our laurels but get out there and start listening to our customers in order find out what is going on."

"Everyone," Tina jumped in unexpectedly, "I've been listening here to Ron talk about the innovation deficiency and the environmental maladaptation sin, and I think these are really issues that are front and center of our existing problem."

Ron decided to let the group air out their thoughts about the process so far, and let Tina throw out her hand grenade into the group.

"I see it a little different, Tina," Melanie quickly jumped on it. "I see that we have wasted half a day so far talking about abstract things that are not fixing our problems. When we walk out of here, we're going to have a bunch of theories and no application."

And then something happened that no one could have imagined. Jerry jumped to Tina's defense.

"I'm normally the group grouch here," he said, "but I think I see where this is going and it's good for us. Now, hell if I know how we're going to pay for it."

With a collective laugh from the group, Ron cleverly decided to take the energy and move them onto the next sin.

Influence Impotence

Ron went back up to the whiteboard again and filled in the last top circle.

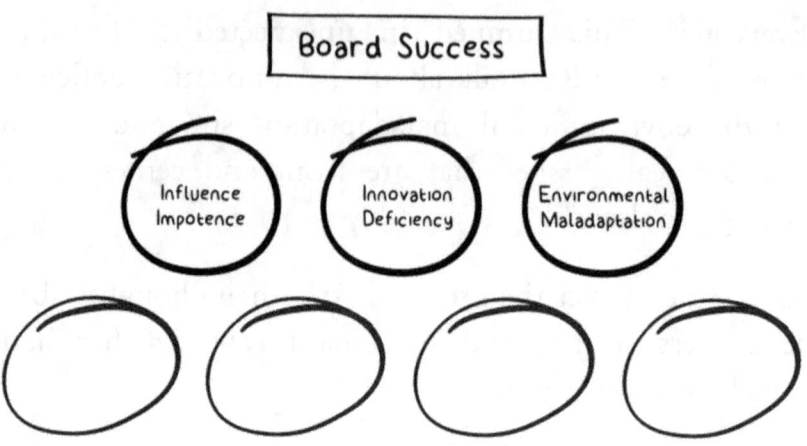

He hardly got a chance to finish writing before the board erupted into laughter.

Jerry was the first to launch in. "There's a blue pill that can fix that one, Ron," he said as he let out a hearty laugh. Ron gave everyone a few moments to let the kindergarten reaction to the word impotence die down.

"So, when we say 'impotence'," he continued, "we actually mean 'unable to perform an action'. And when paired with influence, we talk about the board's ability or inability to open up doors for the organization in terms of contacts. Depending on the type of organization, this influence could come in different shapes and forms. For a corporate board, such as Coppryx, it means access to decision makers in organizations that could be a potential source for new clients. For some organization, like nonprofits for example, it may be access to firms or individuals that are willing to give money. And in some cases it could be access to Federal or State regulatory or legislative bodies in order to influence the outcome of a regulation of a certain bill."

Jerry glanced over the table at Paul, as if they had just come to a wrestling tag-team match. "I've been saying this for years," Jerry started in. "We simply don't have the right personnel on the board and we need people that know people, not just board members that sit and don't do anything."

Paul was slightly more diplomatic: "I serve on other boards that have certain requirements. They have each board director sign annually that we are going to do certain things or make X number of introductions."

"Yeah, but do they actually do it?" Tina turned to Paul with a smirk.

Ron decided to break in. "Okay, let's add the recruiting piece from Jerry to the great ideas list," he said as he wrote it down on the flipchart. "When we talk about influence access," he continued, "I like to use money as an analogy. There are two problems in money - one is not having enough of it and the second is the issue of where to spend it. In the first case we look to create opportunities where we can generate new sources of money in order to afford to buy something. In the second problem, we look at where are the best areas to spend the money that we have. Will you spend it on a new car or will you spend it on a vacation?"

Paul just couldn't resist and jumped in: "I live in Amelia Island in Florida, I would take the car since every day is like a vacation where I live."

The board once again let out an audible chuckle. Ron didn't miss a beat and continued: "So when directors join a board of a particular company, they bring with them a certain amount of influence, or what we call social capital, and they make decisions on where they are going to spend that social capital. So when we talk about influence and access, we mean the directors' capacity or how well connected they are on one hand, and their willingness to use that capital for our organization on the other hand."

This was near and dear to VJ's heart as the nominating committee chair.

"Wait a minute, Ron," VJ interrupted him. "Are you saying that even if we have the world's most connected people on the board that they may or may not use it on our behalf to benefit our organization?"

"Exactly, VJ," Ron replied, nodding his head. "See, that's the problem with board directors, they are in high demand. I bet more than half of you sit on another board."

A number of heads nodded affirmatively.

"So, if every board is going to ask you to do the same thing," Ron continued, "on one hand, you would love to have the CEO of General Electric on your board, but on the other hand, he's probably on so many boards already that in reality you would never get his time or get access to his contacts."

"I have to tell you that I never really thought of it that way," VJ responded.

"So, that aspect of who you bring on," Ron pressed forward, "and what they actually bring to the table, is extremely important. However, what's also equally important is the process of how you will manage influence on the board. And by influence, I'm talking of external influence, outside of the board. The best boards have requirements that directors agree to, before they join it. Nonetheless, where most boards fall short is that they do not effectively or at all enforce these requirements."

"That's exactly what happened on another board I served on," Jerry weighed in. "They brought all of these useless people on the board and even though they said they would do something, they never did jack."

Jerry was politically incorrect 100% of the time but the board was numb to it after so many years.

"So bringing this back home," Ron moved on. "I'd like to do an influence audit and share the results with you."

Ron popped up a small survey again and asked the board directors to rank the quality of their contacts and their willingness to use them for Coppryx. The results appeared up on the screen. As predicted, the survey outcome surprised many in the room.

"As a board," Ron continued, "we can see that we actually have connections to others and have social capital, but our directors are not using them. So, one homework item for us is to figure out what we need to do in order to change the equation."

Melanie had been very quiet through this discussion but finally weighed in: "I give my time and my talent to the board, Ron. I don't think I need to be the chief saleswoman for Coppryx, that's Vanessa's job."

"I'm with Melanie here," Tim added. "When I joined the board, no one told me it was my job to help sell things. If I need to be honest, I'm not sure I would have otherwise joined."

Paul took up his sword and shield and charged in: "That's BS, it's all of our jobs. Your time and your talent isn't enough. I'm sorry, but that's the message here you need to walk away with."

"I'm with Paul on this, VJ uncharacteristically jumped into the fray. "Honestly Tim, you don't even show up for half of the meetings and tell us that your time should be enough?!"

The anger level in the room was clearly escalating. Tina quickly jumped in and tried to placate the situation: "I think Ron is just saying that we need to look into this further. That's all. I'm not sure I'm hearing that we are changing anything at this moment."

Ron was a little surprised by Melanie's willingness to say she wasn't going to do anything else, but didn't' really want to lose ground on the conversation any further. He put down the idea of board influence commitments and enforcement on the great ideas flipchart.

It was getting late in the day and Ron could see that the group was beginning to run out of steam. He turned to Tina to give him the sign that it was time to wrap up and pick up once again tomorrow.

"Thanks everyone for a great day! We will pick up where we left off tomorrow. I know this is a lot to absorb in one day," Tina concluded, as she ended the meeting for the day.

Later in the evening, most of the board directors met up for cocktails at the bar across from the Willard at the Old Ebbitt Grill, one of DC's oldest bars. A series of tables were pulled together.

Tina started the conversation off about the day's work and progress made as the cocktails were being served. "What a great session today, Ron. I really enjoyed it," she said as she tried to start off on a positive note.

Ron was pleased to hear that. Tina's support was a great thing to have on his side, but he also wanted to set expectations accordingly: "Well, the hard work is yet to come Tina. But thank you for the kind words! I appreciate it!"

Jerry was a connoisseur of long-island iced teas. As he gulped down his first one, he said with a devilish grin on his face: "Not half bad, Ron! I mean, don't get me wrong, I still don't like you. Still, not half bad today,"

That was probably the best compliment Jerry ever gave to anyone. However, he quickly changed the subject back to his health woes as the topic changed away from the meeting issues to personal discussions.

"Has anyone seen Melanie?" Tina asked. No one had, as Melanie decided to not come to the bar that evening. Normally, almost all of the directors would get together informally for cocktails. Melanie was frustrated with the discussion over the day and decided that she would boycott the evening in an attempt to express her displeasure.

The rest of the evening, the directors mingled conversations about their personal lives with some discussions meandering back into the various topics from the meeting earlier that day.

Tina announced the last round of drinks, indicating: "We better get some shut-eye as tomorrow is another long Ron-filled day." Everyone laughed, as they left for the evening.

Recruiting Stagnation

As the board directors entered into the room the next morning and wearily filled their coffee mugs, Ron was already up at the front of the board, filling in the newest circle with "recruiting stagnation". Then he placed up two areas - one that read "external", and the other one "internal".

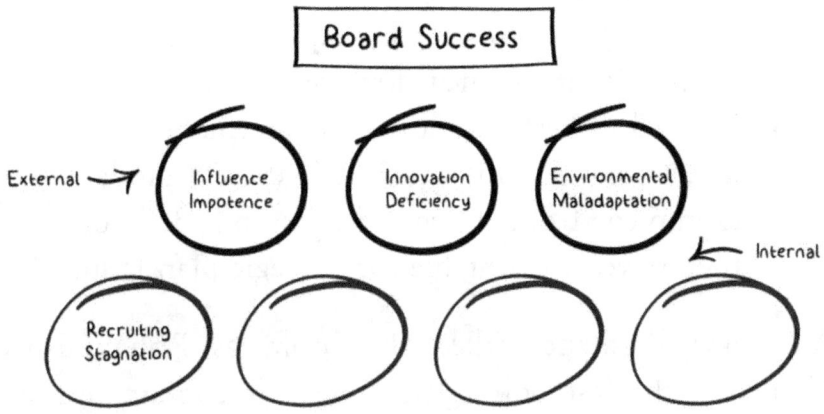

"Before we get started today," Ron announced, "I wanted to set some context first. The three elements we discussed yesterday were really external facing items, in other words pieces of the board that touch the external world more than the items we are about to discuss today, which are more internally focused."

No comments arose from the board, as everyone was still waking up for the early 7 a.m. start. Being way too over-energetic, Ron plowed ahead. "So let's dive in. Our fourth element of corporate board IQ is 'recruiting stagnation'. Stagnation means standing still, or in essence, no movement in our recruiting process. Recruiting stagnation is evident in three primary ways:

1) In-breeding: Boards close themselves off from the outside world and tend to self-perpetuate existing members without adequately considering what

would be best for the organization's needs. These same boards tend to change rules to keep directors in place;

2) Weak Criteria: Boards do not consciously identify personality, skill and expertise criteria, and commitments for new directors;

3) Limited Performance Enforcement- Existing directors are not held to these standards or exempted from these criteria and do not hold themselves accountable for strategic plan failure."

An awkward silence filled the room as Ron finished discussing the last point. Jerry couldn't contain himself: "Great job, Ron! You just pulled the elephant out, placed it in the middle of the table and I can't see a damn thing now because it's literally taking up the entire table."

VJ broke in: "We've been talking about this on the nominating committee recently." He was quickly drowned out by Jerry, who said: "Yeah VJ, we've been talking about this for years on the nominating committee and we have done absolutely nothing".

"Actually, Jerry is right on this one," Paul piled on, "We should have dealt with the board composition issue a long time ago and now we're feeling the pain here. If as a board we took ownership to help grow the market share, we wouldn't have allowed room for our competitor to take it."

Surprisingly, Michael weighed in from the end of the table, as he looked up from his laptop. "Actually, I hate to admit this, but I've not really been involved as a director and I'm one of the people that this elephant is sitting on," he said with a chuckle rising from the other board directors.

"I know there is a lot of frustration about the current sales trend, but let's take a step back," Ron said in an attempt to grab control of the conversation. "Boards are not just made up of business development expertise. We find that highly successful boards know what kind of traits and skills they need and purposefully recruit based on that need. If you know that you lack a certain number of individuals that are willing to help with business development, or you need accounting or legal expertise, then you look for those specific skills. Additionally, successful boards look for certain personality traits to make sure that they are not tilted in one direction. The truth is that you can't have too many argumentative board members or too many folks on a board that don't like conflict, otherwise nothing ever gets done."

"I feel like we've already been moving down this path on the nominating committee," VJ defended himself.

"Right!" Melanie supported VJ. "I think we have good people on the board now and we can address this further with the plans we outlined, but we need to get working on this sales slump problem."

"We haven't been able to resolve this over the past eight years and there is no real path to solve this," Jerry wouldn't let go through, "Who do you think we are kidding?"

"I know we all feel a sense of anxiety about the sales slump, and we will get there," Ron turned to Melanie. "But I'd like to ask for your help in providing me some flexibility to work through the rest of the seven elements. I'm sure we will benefit from discussing them and they will lead to actions in order to address the sales slump."

"Actually, I didn't get to finish my thought here earlier and I think this is important to add at this point," Michael jumped in. "This is hard to admit, but I'm one of the people that shouldn't be here. I'm not very involved and frankly, I don't have the time to be. I should have been honest about this a long time ago and as a board maybe we shouldn't have tolerated it."

Melanie decided to back off given the added support that Ron received from Michael.

Ron let the comment stand and moved in further. "It's important for us to know ourselves before we look outside for others to join the board. Please take a moment to fill out this survey that I just emailed you," Ron continued.

All of the board directors popped up their laptops and started responding to the survey. A look of surprise came over several of the faces of the members as they received their own survey results.

Ron grabbed off a summary of the findings: "Well, board directors can be grouped into several different character types. This does not mean that you are only one type, but rather that you have a dominant style that you prefer in board environments. So on one hand, boards need to know what kind of expertise they need – for example more business development, legal, accounting, or any other specific expertise. But on the other hand, they have to balance the character types."

Melanie could be seen mouthing the abbreviation "WTF" to Jerry, while Jerry had a big smile on his face and couldn't contain himself: "Sabre rattler, huh, perfect!"

A number of directors took turns showing each other their board types until Ron wrestled the meeting back to order: "So, on this board we have whispers, saber rattlers, soothsayers, a couple marines and quite a few backgrounders. What I want everyone to understand is that you wouldn't want just one-character type on the board or it wouldn't function well, therefore you need a diversity of types."

Paul moved back into attack position: "Well from what I see, we have way too many backgrounders that shouldn't be on the bus."

Jerry nodded in vehement agreement. Ron acknowledged Paul's observations and added: "Yes, that's one conclusion, but more importantly we need to know the optimal mix that we want and then work backwards from there. Let's take a few minutes to define the percentage we would want in our optimal board state."

Ron broke the group into 3 teams of eight and asked for each one to develop their composite image for what the optimal board should look like in terms of percentage of board character types and separately - the percentages based on skills (e.g. accounting, legal, business development, human resources, and government relations). Once completed, each team reported back their findings.

Ron pulled the sheets and put them together. "It's interesting that we're not too far off here between the recommendations of the groups, isn't it?" he asked. "Now the hard part is to determine how to achieve the optimal state. We'll put this all together at the end of the day when we prioritize our action items, but the hard part is closing the gap between what we have today versus the optimal state that we want."

Ron walked over to the flipchart and added "close the gap between current and optimal board composition structure" on the action items. Then he felt it was the right time to move onto the next element of corporate board IQ.

Network Misalignment

"Now let's dig a little deeper," Ron said, as he went back up to the whiteboard and filled in the fifth element.

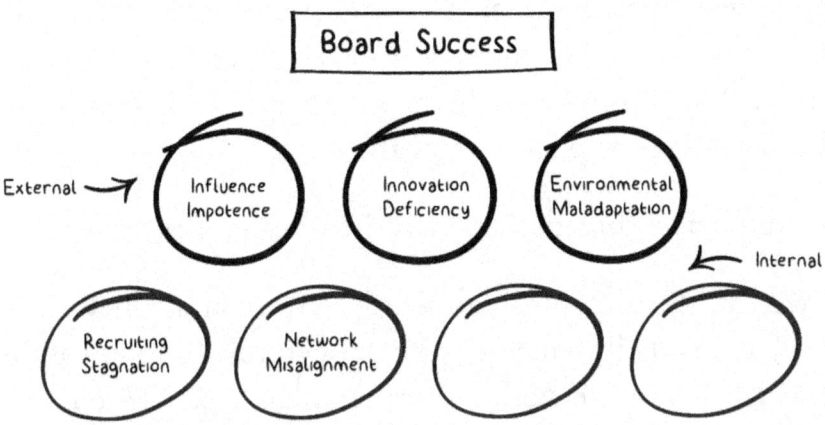

"Have you ever swam in the ocean and noticed that all the waves move in towards the shore," Ron continued, "but sometimes there are undercurrents in the water or riptides that tend to pull you down the beach or even out to the sea? That's exactly what happens in boards of directors as well, but we just are not aware of it often."

"You mean we are swimming upstream without a paddle," Jerry weighed in.

"It can seem like that, Jerry," Ron replied. "Traditionally, when we are at board meetings, we see all the waves crashing on the beach. However, there are many currents that occur hidden beneath the surface. In our board meetings, we see the board room, the reports, our committees and our officers. We perceive this as the formal board and how things get done."

He walked up to the whiteboard and drew a box with the word formal in it. "What we also know is that by the time you get to the board meeting there are many conversations and even decisions that are made long before you walk into the room," Ron explained. These are the currents, right? You cannot see them but they have a significant influence on the operation of the board."

A number of directors nodded their head affirmatively.

"We call this the informal board network and believe it or not, it's actually vital for the proper functioning of the formal board network," Ron emphasized. "When you come on as a new board member, you meet the others on the board and quickly become a part of a team, or a network of board directors. Over time you develop your own relationships with each member and turn to each other for various kinds of information. You may exchange one kind of information or multiple forms of information among each other."

Melanie at this point had busied herself texting on her smartphone. Paul didn't hesitate to give her a nudge with his elbow. She turned to Paul and rolled her eyes.

Ron asked the board to open up another survey and to take a few minutes to fill it out. The survey instrument itself asked several questions, including: names of the board directors; asked which directors they engaged in gossip with; who exchanged information about board tasks; whom they had conflict with; who they trusted the most; who they would turn for advice to; who they would share personal information with. It also asked them to rate those relationships on a scale of 1 to 3 in order to indicate the strength of those relationships.

When done, Ron displayed a map on the screen with the different forms of information. "Now, I de-identified everyone here, so nobody will get a bad rap", he smiled. "But notice how our connections change depending on the type of information we are exchanging with other board directors."

"What's the conflict network?" Kevin asked.

"A conflict network represents individuals who disagree with each other or who have an overall contentious relationship," Ron responded. "When I look at this, I try to determine how large the conflict network is. To be clear, there is always some form of discontent, the trick is making sure that it is not out of hand. When we see a strong current of the conflict network with many players involved, we call that 'Network Misalignment'. Network misalignment is dangerous, as it means there is a strong counter-current. For example, if you want to launch a new initiative and the network is misaligned, this can lead to situations where board meetings become unproductive because the conflict churning in the informal network leads to relationships being formed to perhaps block the new initiative. On the other hand, the conflict network actually could be right and the formal board organization isn't listening to it."

Jerry finally had enough and erupted: "I think this is crap, Ron. I know you put a lot of time into this mojo, but I don't buy this one. Sorry!"

Paul jumped to Ron's defense: "Really Jerry? You don't think there isn't a ton of back-channel stuff that goes on before you step in the room – you're too much!"

As a temporary pause filled the conversation, Melanie felt like most folks were expecting her to say something given her wide scale use of informal channels of communications, however, she remained focused on texting.

Tina tried to allay the conflict: "I think what Ron is telling us is that we just have to make sure that we understand these networks exist and that we want to make sure we're being transparent as a group."

"Right, you're always going to have networks," Ron broke in. "In fact, they kind of serve as a pressure valve for the formal board structure, but there are things highly successful boards do to make sure that these networks are healthy".

Tina called for the afternoon break, but clearly frustrated, Melanie cornered Ron: "I don't see where anything of this is going; you're literally ignoring the biggest problem in the room. We need to move off of this and get to work finally."

Melanie walked off before Ron could respond back. She went to Tina, who was out in the hallway, and said: "Tina, you've got to reign this in and get us focused on why we are here today, or we will waste two days without anything to show for it."

Tina could sense Melanie's frustration with the meeting so far, but wanted to appear sympathetic and encourage her to ride it out. She replied back, "Melanie, I have to admit that I'm not sure exactly where Ron is heading with all of this, but I want to play this out and see where this leads. Again, he's not exactly my speed either but there's some good stuff."

Melanie turned red: "Well, if you ask me, it's a big time-waster."

As Melanie walked off, Tina approached Ron. "I hope you know what you're doing, Ron. Some of the natives are restless," she said with a half-smile.

"I know, Tina, but we cannot get to change without getting uncomfortable," Ron replied.

She decided that the die was cast at this point and it was best to allow Ron to continue.

Paul approached Tina during the break and grabbed the seat next to him at the table. "You have to break a few eggs to make an omelet, you know that," Paul said, as he patted Tina on the shoulder.

"Just one more meeting as chair and I'm done," she said with a smile.

Ron decided to pull back on digging deeper on network misalignment, as he sensed that the major problem at the moment was solving some of the critical recruiting challenges that the board faces. Instead, he opted to move forward with the next element.

Accountability Shortage

By the time the group had re-caffeinated and gathered themselves, it was 3 p.m. in the afternoon.

"When does happy hour start," Jerry chimed in before things got started.

"Forget it Jerry!" Tina responded. "We still have real work to do this time."

While everyone was getting settled back in, Ron was hard at work filling in the third "internal" bubble with "lack of accountability".

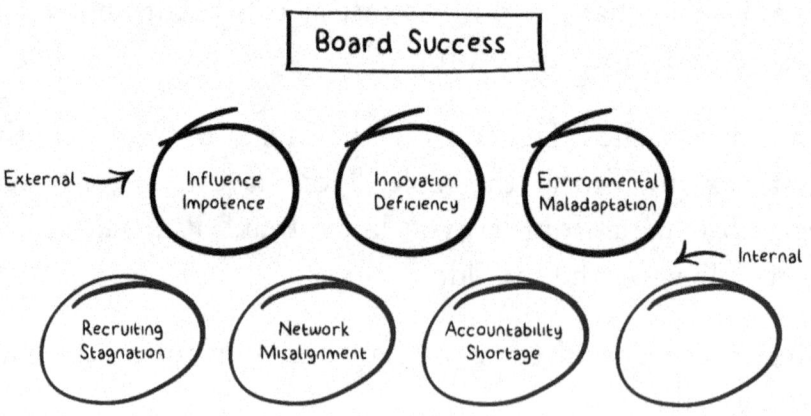

"When we think of accountability," he started, "we think about holding staff accountable for goals and behaviors. And that's a critical part of this bubble. We should not think of this as only a staff issue. Most boards understand as part of accountability that they have legal and fiduciary responsibilities, which are critically important. However, as a board, we have to hold ourselves accountable not only for the success, but for failures of the organization as well."

"The board has accountability today for the organization's success," Kevin weighed in, as he felt that Ron was singling him out. "I have a ton of metrics that I report back to the board quarterly and they hold me accountable for organizational performance."

Ron could sense the tension in Kevin's voice and decided to pivot his approach to make sure he didn't lose Kevin: "You're completely right, Kevin! The CEO is accountable for organizational performance. But the board needs to make sure we are measuring the right things. And accountability isn't just on your shoulders, Kevin, it's on all of us as agents of the board."

"You're spot on, Ron," Paul jumped into the fray. "Why in the hell didn't we see all of this coming with the drop in our sales figures until now? We should have had better intelligence and see this was coming. Instead, we just tend to passively accept sales figures that are already dated by the time we get them."

Paul was clearly frustrated with the lack of transparency around the metrics, but Ron was concerned not to let the conversation devolve into finger pointing back at Kevin.

"I don't think we want to pin the tail on the donkey here," Ron continued, "but there is a logical line to some of our current problems that we didn't see coming. In the world of performance metrics, we call these leading versus lagging measures. When Kevin reports the number of units sold or the revenue generated, those are lagging indicators which we only realize after a certain outcome. However, leading indicators are those that are indicative of something that will happen in the future. For example, how many prospects are we talking with currently, or purchase orders that are outstanding at the time. Again, both types of metrics are important, but the trick is to manage the balance between them."

"I guess you're trying to say that we didn't have any leading indicators to know what kind of problems we were going to encounter," VJ jumped in.

"Right, that's one of the issues we had," Ron nodded, "namely, we probably knew this well in advance but we didn't have the right indicators. If you're flying a plane and you don't have a radar system in place, sometimes flying by eyesight can lead you into a mountain."

Then Ron went to the whiteboard and drew the following diagram.

While he was busy doing that, he stated: "Now listen everyone, I didn't invent this. You probably saw this when you went to your first business course in college. However, I put this up here because I have found that organizations tend to be really good at measuring tactics and strategies, but much worse in measuring goals, mission and vision. How do we know that we actually are achieving what we are setting out to do if we cannot measure it?"

"How exactly do you measure our vision to be the best medical device supplier in the universe, Ron?" Jerry jumped in.

"I guess we have to determine how to measure best and against who," VJ added.

"Okay, so let's take a few minutes and do just that," Ron intercepted them. Once again he broke the board up into three teams and had them brainstorm on leading and lagging indicators for the current vision, mission and goals.

Kevin was extremely concerned about this part of the conversation, as he could see a rash of new metrics being shoved down for him to have to feed back to the board.

"I'm worried that this is going to be a ton of work on Vanessa, Jimmy and I to have to feed this metric beast," Kevin noted nervously.

A few heads nodded around the room.

"Kevin, I understand your concern on the workload here," Tina jumped in. "Maybe we need to look at all of our metrics to see the ones we really need and if we could drop some."

Ron was happy to see Tina attempting to help sort through the problem. "Yes, I think we ask each team to tackle that as well in your break-out groups," he added.

When the groups came back together, they assembled a "start doing" and "stop doing" list of leading and lagging for the vision, mission and goals. Together, each board director was asked to rank them and what was left was a relative weight of each of the metrics.

"We now have general agreement and ideas on how to best structure metrics for each of these areas," Ron weighed in. "And conversely, we prioritized some of these pretty low as well, which begs the question if we even need them."

"I think we need to get these metrics down to a reasonable set that give us good information about what we can expect and what is happening, but not a ton of various metrics," Paul suggested.

Through further discussion, the board settled on their top 2 leading and lagging metrics to track for the mission, vision and goals. Ron now pivoted the conversation to accountability.

"Kevin was right earlier when he made the comment that he was in the hot seat and held responsibility for performance. Nonetheless, as a board, what do we do to stay focused on our strategic plan?" Ron asked.

"Well, our strategic plan gets pulled off the shelf once a year, gets dusted off, reviewed and put back on the shelf," Paul dove in.

"Come on Paul!" Tina was ticked. 'You know that's not exactly how it works."

"I provide an executive report at every board meeting and talk about where we are with our marketing, financials and sales," Kevin noted. "It's not like we are not talking about the strategic plan."

"I think the point here is, it is one thing to talk about performance," Ron jumped in, "but it's quite another thing to talk about the strategic plan and whether the strategies we defined are working or not." Ron made a pause and tried to change the conversation: "What other ways can we engage the board on accountability?"

"We can assign individuals to specific goals," Melanie suggested, and Ron nodded in agreement.

"We can conduct an annual appraisal of the board's success in advancing the strategic plan," VJ added, and Ron nodded once again.

"Both are great ideas," he noted.

The board spent considerable time identifying the various areas that could use a "board champion" and Ron walked back up to the flipchart and jotted down the following as an action items: "Create board appraisal and assign board champions". It was getting late in the day and Ron decided to move the group onto the seventh and last element of corporate board IQ- "Power Imbalance".

Power Imbalance

Everyone filtered back in the room after grabbing cookies that were placed out on the side of the room. The energy level was fading, as everyone waited for their glucose levels to kick in with the cookies.

"Everyone is doing a great job here and I promise I'll get everyone home by midnight," Ron announced with a smile. A half-hearted laugh and groan fell over the group as he went up to the whiteboard to fill in the last circle.

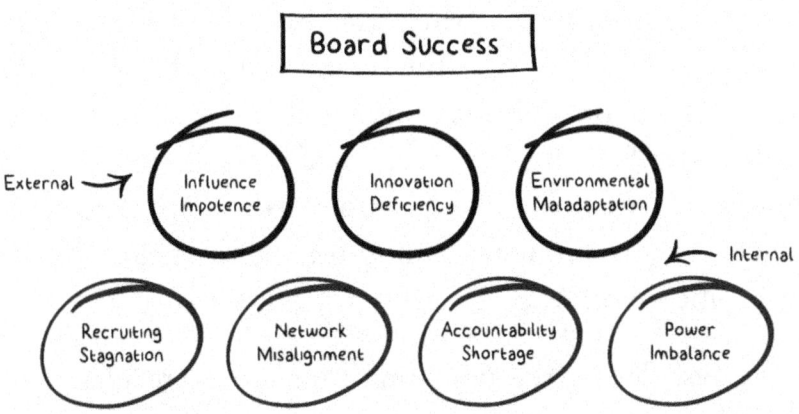

"'Power Imbalance' is one that most boards never fully consider, but often feel its impact," Ron emphasized. "Boards operate in either a top-down, bottom-up, or sideways," Ron surmised.

A number of board directors looked at each other with confusion.

"Okay, I'm thoroughly confused, Ron, as to what in the world that even means?" Tina asked finally.

Ron smiled and went to the whiteboard and drew up a traditional board model.

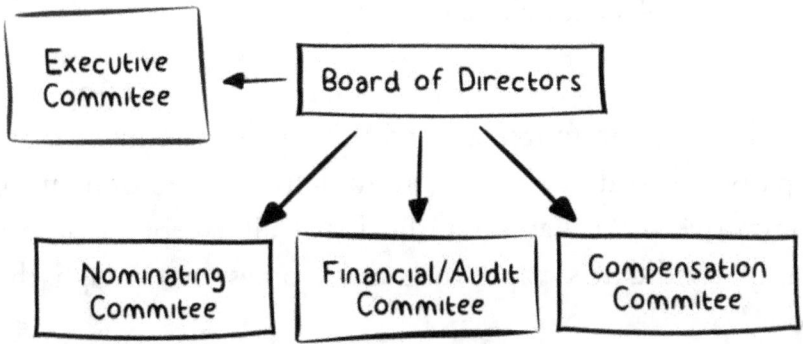

"'Power Imbalance' is when the board gives too much power to one group over the other, leading to poor board performance or disenfranchisement by directors," Ron explained. "So when we say 'top-down', 'bottom-up', or 'side-ways', we are talking about where the power is concentrated within the committees of the board. Let me give some examples:

Side-ways: The executive committee meets regularly and most decisions are made there; Result - the full board feels like they have no say in anything;

Bottom-up: The board committees do most of the work and provide reports back to the full board of directors. Result - the full board feels like they are there to rubber stamp decisions made by committees;

Top-down: The board does all of the work and does not delegate down to committees or delegates; Result - committees feel like they do not make a difference and are not engaged.

"Each version of power imbalance has a challenge associated with it, so it's up to each board to identify the right mix," Ron concluded.

VJ felt passionate about this, as the head of the nominating committee and added: "This feels like we are top-down board to me. I've always felt like the nominating committee really has no authority at all except to rubber stamp candidate's paperwork that comes in through the door."

"You can say that again," Jerry nodded vigorously.

Melanie sat silent through the discussion on power balance and once again preferred tending to her smartphone.

Ron took a straw poll of the group with a show of hands to see what the group thought best reflected their board and the results confirmed what VJ had noted a minute ago.

"I don't recall us ever discussing whether we have the right committees here on the board," Paul asked.

"I think we did many years ago, Paul," Tina responded, "but to be honest, I don't think it has been done recently."

Ron intercepted the idea and noted: "Let's capture that on the great ideas log." Then he jotted on the flipchart the following: "Review board committee structure - to determine if we have it right".

It was now 6 p.m. and Ron could see that everyone was practically comatose at this point. However, he was not quite done yet. He needed to make one more push.

Wrap-Up

Ron went back over to the "great ideas" log and pulled all of the ideas that were generated over the past two days.

"Okay, now the hard job is solving problems rather than just identifying them," he said. "I'd like to go through the challenges and great ideas and come up with a prioritization plan, and how we are going to tackle them."

A noticeable groan emerged from the group, as everyone jumped up to grab some coffee.

"I think we just set up a conference call to discuss the next steps, Ron. We're bushed."

Paul shook his head no and jumped in: "We need to get to some concrete action steps before dispersing. I'm going to recommend we pull an all-nighter if necessary to get this done."

Tina concurred with Paul and suggested that the board spend the next two hours to come up with an action plan.

Ron entered the data gathered from the great ideas and the key challenges on an online survey. Then he proceeded to have the board vote electronically and displayed the information up on the projection screen.

"Based on the results," Ron started, "the green dots indicate the elements of corporate board IQ that we're going to focus on. I'd like to recommend that the same group that was focused on recruiting stagnation, to work on influence impotence. I believe in this case they are closely related to each other."

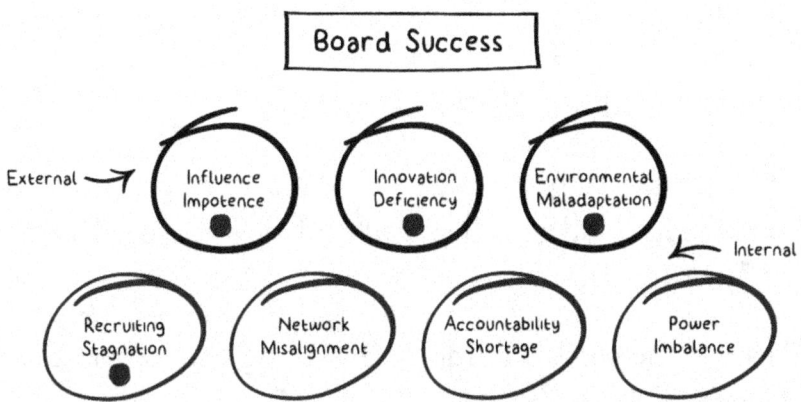

Tina made an observation: "I think we need another meeting to get to concrete action relatively quickly. I know this isn't popular but can we schedule a fly-in for a one-day meeting to see if we can get some action on these items?"

"You must not think that we don't have a day job, do you Tina?" Jerry responded. Melanie again sat quiet, preoccupied with her phone.

"We don't have time to wait a quarter," Paul was the first to agree. "I say we do it and in fact, plan two days in case it takes that long."

"I cannot get that much time away from the office at all," Rachel replied from the end of the table.

Tina was determined to move forward and set a follow-up meeting for 6 weeks from now. The board was broken up into teams about the key four elements of corporate board IQ and were charged with coming up with an action plan to correct the four elements and evaluating the "great ideas" lists in each of the categories. Kevin agreed to staff the calls and also work with each team to develop a budget as needed to address the items.

With that the retreat concluded. Tina walked up to Ron: "You weren't kidding when you said now the hard work is next."

"Turning the ship is harder than seeing the iceberg ahead sometimes," Ron retorted.

He wished he could have gotten further with the board, but knew this was important groundwork to what really needed to happen.

Chapter 2:
Turning Point

Over the next several weeks, each of the assigned three "sin taskforces" as they became known met weekly for approximately two hours to develop plans that would be presented at the next board meeting.

The room at the Hyatt in Tysons Corner was freshly built and bolted alongside a mega-mall on the outskirts of Washington DC. The black mid-rise tower certainly wasn't the tallest building in the area but was still impressive against the stark white contrast of the mall to which it was attached. Kevin liked to come over the evening ahead of time to meet with Tina and other board directors that may also arrive early.

Around 5 p.m. Kevin walked into the restaurant Earl's, which was adjacent to the hotel across a sky bridge. Earl's had a hip urban vibe to it with soaring ceilings and a décor best described as 1950's art deco meets 21st century. Kevin grabbed one of the back semi-circular booths and ordered a gin and tonic. Tina came in with Paul and Ron.

All three squeezed into the booth. As everyone settled in and ordered cocktails, the requisite chit-chat kicked up about the weather, families and personal issues that were normal for the start of the board meeting. Kevin always thought that it helped make business easier to discuss once you knew where everyone stood personally.

Tina was the first to break the ice between personal issues and business. "So how's progress been on the corporate board IQ taskforces?" she asked pointedly.

"Slow but steady," Kevin replied. "Actually, steady and unsteady," Kevin revised his statement.

"So what's the problem?" Paul asked.

"Two of the groups have been making pretty good progress," Kevin reported. "I think we'll be pleased in the meeting coming up with the results, but the recruiting group is just not moving."

Kevin was sad to say this, as VJ was a close friend of his, but he had noticed that even though VJ was assigned to lead the team, he was unable to make any traction on any new groundbreaking ideas around recruiting and influence.

"Boards tend to smell insincerity in the air and if we're not convicted about making a change, VJ's going to get eaten for breakfast," Paul turned to Kevin. "I personally think we need to go big or go home."

"This part is really frustrating because we know we need to make changes but sometimes things just get stuck," Ron interrupted. "Let's work with VJ to see what the issue is and help him get unstuck."

After the second round of cocktails, VJ checked into the hotel. A few minutes later he came over to the bar and joined the rest of the board members. He looked unusually somber. Tina tried to dig a bit: "So I hear you're having some fun on those calls to discuss recruiting and influence?"

That was all the prompting that VJ needed: "You know, Tina, I told you early on in the year that this nominating thing and now this team is a toothless dog. I can't get anything done and I end up spending time arguing with Melanie about what problem we are trying to fix."

"What problem are we trying to fix?" Ron asked with a smile.

VJ huffed in frustration, took another swig of his drink and replied: "We get hung up on the same issues of how to restructure the board and does it apply to existing board directors or not."

"I don't think that's what the problem is," Ron turned to VJ.

VJ's face filled beet red, as he was about to jump over the table at Ron.

"I think the problem you have is that Melanie is actively sabotaging efforts to change our recruiting effort," Ron said. Then he turned to Tina and continued: "And I also think you're the only one that can fix it."

Tina looked noticeably uncomfortable at that moment.

"He's saying you need to get rid of her, Tina," Paul offered.

"I know what he means, Paul," Tina replied."

"You're in the best position to do it since you're chair and you're heading out," Paul added. "Who else is going to do it otherwise?"

Tina knew that Paul was right but didn't like the idea of telling Melanie that she would have to step off the board. Grudgingly, Tina agreed he would talk to her after tomorrow's meeting.

Explosions

As directors entered the room to take their seats, Melanie came in, hardly said a word and just sat at the far end of the table. Meanwhile, Jerry showed up with a bit of a smile on his face, which was quite unusual.

"Audit season is about to start, ladies and gentlemen," Jerry announced. "I'm sure everyone is as excited as I am."

Jerry had been elected last year to the treasurer position of the board and took that role like a duck in water.

"Not half as excited as you are, but ready nonetheless," Tina responded.

Jerry went over and grabbed two big cookies and a Coke. "My wife has been driving me crazy with this diet stuff," Jerry grumbled as he returned back to his seat.

As the personal conversations died down, Tina opened the meeting up and turned to VJ to lead the first corporate board IQ taskforce group on recruiting stagnation.

"I admittedly didn't get very far on this folks," VJ started in. "We had a hard time scheduling our team and didn't get any real traction forward on this. We revised the old requirements for the directors and came up with a commitment form to use. But frankly, we didn't make a lot of progress."

Ron was disappointed, albeit not surprised as he knew that issues around board composition posed some of the most challenging changes, as they required groups to have to take a hard look at themselves.

Paul jumped in: "I cannot believe that we have an issue so important as this one and you all come back with watered down recommendations that we've been studying for years."

VJ fell on the sword: "Really the responsibility is mine, as I was appointed to be the leader of this group. I just didn't push hard enough."

"For me it was just a timing issue," Rachel chimed in. "We didn't have enough time to get the work done as my day job was freezing me."

Melanie looked up from her phone and added: "I don't know what problem we are still trying to fix. So why are you surprised that we don't have any major recommendations?"

A moment of uncomfortable silence fell across the room as eyes moved back over to Tina. She decided to make her move and said: "Melanie, I think it's time to stop denying that we have an issue here. As a director, we cannot tolerate having you continually block progress on this topic. If you cannot see the reasons we need to make the change, then perhaps you should recuse yourself from the nominating committee."

One could have heard a pin hit the floor at this very moment, as all of the directors sat stunned. But Tina was not done: "And VJ, you were given the responsibility to lead this group which was critically important. If you couldn't do it or find time, you should have told me and I would have found someone else."

Melanie and VJ were stunned as they had never seen Tina be so straightforward before. Melanie could not believe that Tina would do this to her and embarrass her in such a way in front of the entire board.

Tina called for a break and went over to Melanie, who was busy packing up: "Melanie, I just want to…"

Before she could finish Melanie cut in: "I will not put up with such treatment. If you want this board seat, then you can have it. I'm done." Melanie wasted no time and walked out of the room in a hurry.

Meanwhile, Kevin was playing damage control with VJ on his way back from the bathroom. VJ was sullen. "Kevin, I didn't really want to take on this nominating thing from the beginning, and frankly, I screwed this up," he said.

Kevin suggested that someone else partner with him to see if they could get things moving faster. At that same moment, Tina walked over towards them.

"Well, that didn't go well", Tina noted and then turned to VJ. "I'm sorry VJ for coming down so hard on you, but…"

VJ cut her off: "But you need to hold people accountable and I did a pretty pitiful job of the task assigned to me. I realize that."

"Well, yes," Tina responded.

"You Know Tina," VJ continued, "one of the problems I have realized here, is me actually. I've been here for eight years and outside of being a good friend to Kevin and you, I'm not sure whether I'm really bringing anything fresh to the table."

Kevin jumped in to defend the contributions that he had made in the past but VJ interrupted him.

"Hear me out, Kevin," he continued, "I'm not looking to be patted on the shoulder. Maybe I didn't get around to moving this discussion forward because I'm one of the people that shouldn't be here."

Kevin and Tina listened intently.

"Truth hurts sometimes. Tina, I'm going to resign after the next board meeting and that'll fee up the slot. You should pick Ron to carry the recruiting work. He's the right workhorse," VJ concluded.

Tina nodded affirmatively and Kevin ultimately agreed with his request to carry the work forward. As they walked back into the room, Tina thanked VJ for his leadership and frankness.

The group re-convened from the break with the board noticeably uncomfortable having witnessed Tina's tirade and Melanie storming out of the room.

Environmentally Centered

The board shouldered on and continued the work. Paul led the environmental maladaptation group and had obviously done an incredible job by all measures. He was armed with survey results from existing clients and client prospects about Coppryx and the marketplace.

The data confirmed what Kevin had expected but also offered new insights around the loss of market share.

"So Kevin and I looked at the survey data," Paul started, "and we found that actually, our competitor's product, while newer technology, isn't exactly our biggest issue. It's actually that they offer better service than we do."

Paul outlined ways that NecroTech had listened to their customers to inform their product enhancements: "We're being killed on the fact that we don't know our customers as well as we thought we did."

Paul had noted that his team had now created focused groups and was already convening them to evaluate how Coppryx's services and delivery. He also noted that the design features that the competitor was touting over Coppryx were in fact "small" improvements to the interface that could be relatively easy to change.

"Just remember that technical innovation is short lived and we can address things like that pretty quickly," Ron added.

"One thing we also realized through all of this was that we have no client representation on the Coppryx board," Paul noted. "I'd like to add that to the great ideas list."

Many members of the board nodded in agreement, as Ron added it up on the flipchart.

Paul began to outline his plan between now and the next board meeting in 8 weeks to continue the work of the client focus groups and to develop a series of long term recommendations that would require board funding to executive and short-term fixes that would be implemented immediately without the need for board action.

"I'm still very nervous that this is going to cost too much money," Jerry weighed in.

"I understand, Jerry," Paul dove in, "that's why we will prioritize our recommendations back to the board."

Kevin noted that he was coordinating with Paul on this and was going to visit more clients' sites and prospects in order to raise the company's market visibility. He was also having his sales team members to go out and visit customer sites to see what it was like to "walk in their shoes."

As Paul completed his report, the mood lightened on the board as the morning's recruiting train wreck was moving into the background now.

Next up, Ron got up to present on the innovation deficiency groups' findings. He referenced the "great ideas" log from the last meeting and noted that the effort to spur innovation is not a fast turn, but starting to make these changes will lead the "fertile pasture" for innovation to develop.

Ron presented the first finding: "First, we will use one of our retreats annually to invite cross-industry expertise to join us for various topics to find out how they handle similar problems in their particular sector and see what kinds of lessons we can learn from them. This is important, as it allows us an opportunity to see things in a different light then we usually do."

"Are you sure it's going to be useful to hear a plumber tell us about his difficulties," Paul asked with a skeptical look on his face.

"Probably we don't go with plumbing, Paul," Ron laughed, "but I'm thinking more like sister industries to healthcare - the airlines for example, transportation, or financial services would be good comparisons in this case."

"I actually really like that idea," Tim spoke up, "as I would imagine topics like customer acquisition or even productive development cut across multiple industries."

"We are going to ask a client or an industry expert to brief us on teleconferences 4X per year to discuss what impact it may have on our product," Ron pressed ahead. "This will allow the board to be more in touch with what is going on external to us, and to gather information that may help us make better investment decisions in the future."

Surprisingly, Jerry nodded his head yes and responded: "That makes a lot of sense, usually we just come here and get board reports thrown at us."

Finally, Ron suggested that an R&D department is to be expanded at Coppryx. Kevin was waiting for Ron to suggest this and threw his support behind it: "For years, Coppryx has been able to ride the wave, but we need to work on the next generation of our product and services now. I think the expansion is necessary."

Jerry, being the ever-present treasurer felt obliged to jump in: "As long as this R&D department doesn't come up with new ways to spend money."

"Of course they're going to spend money, Jerry," Paul countered, "but bear in mind that they're going to have to justify it like any other organization does."

"Actually sort of yes and sort of no, Paul," Ron added. "Really, we need to think about this the same way entrepreneurs do. There is an idea, a business plan and an investment strategy. If we can show a good plan and a solid rational for investment, of course we need to invest. But with innovation it's not certain. In fact, we will invest in many innovations that may ultimately fail or form together years later to be successful."

Jerry went back to his old self: "Well, I want to see old-fashioned financial projections that aren't just guesses."

"Jerry, if you don't trust financial projections," Tina tried to back Ron, "what do you actually want - blood and DNA samples?"

An audible laugh filled the room. Jerry decided to back-off.

Ron noted that between now and the next meeting, they would get the new program in place and would formulate the budget request for the R&D department creation.

With the final report in, Tina was quick to close the meeting in order to get everyone on their afternoon flights. She noted that at the next board meeting they would want to make sure that the board was focused on implementation reports rather than interim status reports on the ideas that were generated. Kevin noted that he would follow-up with key actions from each group that were identified and reminded that the existing taskforce leaders would champion these at the next board meeting.

Change of Guard

As the retreat closed, Kevin scheduled dinner that evening with Tina and VJ to discuss the chair position for the following year. Tina had served in this role for almost four years and her tenure was finally coming to an end.

Kevin picked up Tina from her office and drove out to the Ruth Chris in Tysons Corner, which was close to their homes in Northern Virginia. They walked into the plush bar and had a seat on the rather uncomfortable sofas in the bar.

Tina took her first sip from the gin and tonic she had just ordered and placed it gently on the table, as she turned to Kevin and said: "Kevin, that was a hell of a ride for me as chair for the past two years. I'm afraid that if you had told me what I was really going to get into, to be entirely honest I'm not really sure that I would have accepted. I can't believe how fast the time went by here. I was never really quite comfortable in the role," Tina admitted.

Kevin assured her that she was exactly what the organization had needed at the time and was grateful for her friendship and leadership. He expressed his concerns and reminded Tina that there was a hard task ahead of them, namely trying to determine her successor, since no one had wanted to step up to the chair-elect role during the last election cycle.

As if on cue, Paul came in through the front door and dusted the rain off his black overcoat and sat next to Kevin. "Sorry I'm late folks, the traffic was a beast today."

"We've got a head start on cocktails, Paul, I hope you don't mind," Tina smiled. She made a short pause allowing Paul to order a drink and turned to him once again: "I know you told us that you wanted to step down, but you've been such an invaluable board director for years. I was hoping that you would consider taking over my role as chair, given your experience in running the nominating committee and long tenure on the board."

Paul took a big gulp from his gimlet and casted an awkward smile back over to Tina.

"I'm honored, Tina, I really am," he stammered, "but I'm not the right person for the job."

Tina's smile quickly gave way to a look of concern, which she could not contain.

"I don't mean this with any disrespect," Paul continued, "I'm enjoying my retirement and I just don't see myself taking this role on. I actually have been thinking that in a year or two that I might step away from the board to make room for new blood at some point."

As she was listening to VJ, Tina's face turned two shades whiter. She had always assumed that he was the presumptive nominee for the position.

"Paul, do you mean 'no' at this moment, or 'no' forever?" Kevin chimed in, hoping that some humor might make the situation a little lighter and that there was still an opportunity to convince Paul to change his mind.

"Listen guys, we've been friends for quite some time and I have to tell you, we have a tough road ahead of us. I'm just not up for all of the ass kicking and politicking," Paul noted with a tone of intensity and then added: "I'm retired officially, and the hardest thing I want to be challenged with is my golfing handicap."

"Crap, Paul! I think you're just making excuses," Tina said, visibly upset.

"Tina, don't take this personal, please!" Paul responded. "I don't mean it that way. I'm just telling you that we need some real tough leadership going forward and I'm not the guy. However, I think we already do have the right guy on the board - a bit unorthodox - but we have him."

Tina turned away from Paul's serious stare and looked at Kevin, whose silence was clearly deafening through the exchange.

"Who did you have in mind that's unorthodox? Melanie?" Tina quipped.

Paul gave her a thin smile as he took another sip from his cocktail before he continued: "No, not even close. I think we need to tap Ron on the shoulder here for this job."

"You're kidding' Tina continued her assault. "We cannot place a board director in his first year as the chair. He doesn't know the first thing about Coppryx's operations and he's not yet familiar with the culture of this organization. Besides, there are so many others that have been around much longer and would be entitled to run," Tina surmised.

"Listen Tina, there's all sorts of reasons why this sounds like a bad idea," Paul explained, "but frankly, when you look at the options…Yes, it's crazy and unorthodox, but it might just make it the right course of action."

The dinner wrapped up with Tina begrudgingly making peace with the concept that she would set up a meeting with Ron.

To Be or Not to Be

Approximately a week later, Tina arranged a lunch meeting with Ron at the local Silver Diner. She got to the diner a few moments early, dressed in a dark gray pencil shirt and white blouse, and used the time to jot down some notes. Ron came in exactly on time, wearing his classic look of blue jeans and polo shirt, accessorized with flip fops on.

"Hey there Tina, nice to see you!" Ron shook hands with Tina, as she struggled to squeeze between the table and the back of the red booth seat.

"My pleasure, Ron! Thanks for meeting me on such short notice," she smiled.

Tina expressed her appreciation of the fact that Ron had joined the board. She spent a significant amount of time telling Ron about the history of the organization and the board. Tina felt awkward about having this conversation and tended to dance around the issue for quite some time, as she made an effort to steer the conversation towards discussing how great and fulfilling it had been for her to have served as the chair.

Finally, after about 45 minutes, Tina built up his confidence and asked Ron if he would be willing to take over as the chair of the board.

Ron sat back in his chair, clearly stunned, "Do you always welcome first term board directors by asking them if they want to be the chair?" he asked with a devilish grin.

"Desperate times call for desperate measures, Ron. I've heard you say that before," Tina responded with a smile on her face.

"Indeed," Ron replied. "But what makes you think I'm the right person for the job?"

"Actually it was Paul's idea, Ron. He's been very impressed with your leadership and really appreciated your vision in the retreat that we held. He and I both agree that if Coppryx is going to survive, it's going to need a chair that can make the hard decisions and get the group behind them."

Ron spent the next two hours peppering Tina with a series of questions about the board, the challenges and the direction that the organization needed to take.

"Listen Tina, I'm interested in the position," he added, "but in order for me to pull off this turnaround, we are going to have to make difficult changes. We must look like the organization that we want to be and the board has to lead the organization, not just follow like we are doing right now, Tina."

Tina couldn't help but feel like she was being attacked and responded back: "Ron, it's not all bad, we've done a pretty good job over the past ten years and have good people on the board."

Ron listened intently before speaking: "Tina, I'm not attacking you or the past, but frankly, mediocrity is the enemy of progress. We have to reimagine ourselves, and by 'ourselves', I mean not only our strategies and plans, but the board itself. If we want to survive and thrive, we have to become much more nimble and forward-facing than we are today."

Tina backed down, as to not inflame things further with Ron, but did not completely buy into the fact that an entire overhaul was needed. She reminded herself once again, "only one more meeting left as the chair."

Ron and Tina finished up their lunch talking about the various problems further, with an understanding that Ron, Tina and Kevin would meet-up over at Coppryx's headquarters prior to the next board retreat in order to lay out a plan of attack.

Chapter 3:
Lasting Changes

The final board meeting for Tina Hernandez was now at hand, as Tina's flight arrived at Washington-Dulles airport. On the plane, Tina reflected about her time at Coppryx as the Chair of the board. She was feeling mentally ready to step down. In the recent moths she had caught herself numerous times imagining all of the things she would do with her new found free time.

Tina thought about turning the reigns over to Ron. "After all," she thought to herself, "the best gift I can give the board is a great successor." And while she had reservations about Ron's tenure and youth, she felt that he was the right candidate.

Tina's willingness at the end to step up and hold both Melanie and VJ accountable would prove to be a significant change that would alter the future of

Coppryx's board. Additionally, over the past six weeks, Tina and Kevin agreed that they would not fill Melanie's seat or VJ's soon-to-be vacant seat, at least not until Ron took over and they had a better idea of how they envision restructuring the board.

That evening, back in Tysons Corner at Earl's, Tina, Kevin and Ron met up for cocktails at the bar. They greeted each other warmly and spoke about their own personal lives. Ron finally asked Tina: "Are you ready for the big transition?"

"Indeed I am, Ron," Tina laughed, "but the real question we have here is 'are you ready'?"

The three sat down and discussed further the progress that each of the teams had made since the last meeting and tried to outline how tomorrow's meeting would go.

Board Structure Shake-Up

The next morning, the directors came in on time for the 7 a.m. meeting. This was the annual board meeting where the new officers were appointed for the year. However, given Melanie's departure and VJ's impending, it was decided to appoint the new Chair first and complete the structural changes before recruiting new directors or appointing new officers.

Tina welcomed the board members and moved quickly to entertain a motion to accept Ron as the new chair of the board. Running unopposed, Ron was quickly elected and the board gave him a round of applause.

The newly appointed chairman did not waste any time and as the next order of business Ron continued the work of the "corporate board IQ taskforces". He started with the "recruiting and influence" group that he had taken over from VJ at the last meeting. Ron indicated that the group had changed tact and expanded its focus. He also noted that the group had changed its composition in order to include two outside CEOs and a client.

Afterwards, VJ presented a new board structure that capped the board at 9 directors. Then he presented a matrix of skills, personalities and expertise of what those 9 directors should look like, along with new annual board commitment criteria. He showed how the existing board lined up against the new criteria and board structure.

Nervous looks crept in, particularly from Rachel, Tim and Michael who had not been very active on the board.

"I've been saying it for years," Jerry was the first to lead the charge, "and now, we are here to pay the piper. I'm in."

Paul and VJ both jumped in behind the new structure and while there were a few questions, the surprise came from Tim and Michael.

"Frankly, I'm not happy with the new model," Michael started, "as this pretty much means I lose my board seat. I don't think these participation criteria are really fair," he concluded.

Jerry stayed true to himself as always and didn't hesitate to move in for the kill: "Why? Maybe because you wouldn't be able to meet them?"

"Come on, Jerry!" Michael erupted. "That's just not fair, I've had some crises that were unavoidable."

"Actually, I'm on the other side of this," Tim followed up. "As I mentioned before, I haven't been plugged in and frankly, I don't deserve to be on this board. I think the criteria make sense and it's time to implement something like this, even if it means I lose my seat."

"The point here, Michael," VJ jumped into the fray, "is not to make you feel bad, but we all are busy and while there are occasional exceptions, it's not fair that we don't continue to enforce these criteria. We're giving folks free passes and they are not contributing to the success of the board."

"I'm one of them, I have to confess," Rachel spoke up, "I've not been able to juggle this well enough and if we all want to be entirely honest, the truth is I probably won't be able to make the commitment. I don't like to say it, but that's how it really is."

Ron knew self-interest was the main reason why the board tended to not make any progress on recruitment and structure topics. He felt somewhat surprised, but at the same time he was truly impressed with the self-reflection of some of the less participatory board directors.

"Thank you for the comments on this!" Ron followed up. "None of this is meant to be personal attacks. Our duty is to Coppryx. We all have to be honest with ourselves and each other. Recruiting stagnation is one of the elements because boards typically are not honest with each other and allow this to go unchecked. The board would begin the recruiting process based on the new structure and criteria."

By the end of the discussion, Rachel and Tim agreed to surrender their seats now, and Michael would surrender his at the end of the next year to make room for new directors that matched the new structure and criteria.

Kevin himself had mixed feelings about the changes, and while he was excited about the refreshing energy the new board directors would bring, he also knew it meant more work to indoctrinate a new board. He was losing friends, someone like VJ, who had been a great confidant and ally over the years. Nonetheless, he had the firm belief that he didn't want to get in the way of the progress and remained silent through most of the discussion. However, it was the next point that Ron brought up to the conversation that invoked the wrath of the board.

Board Performance Evaluations

Ron noted that "one recommendation our recruiting and influence taskforce wishes to make is to implement an annual board peer review program, where board directors will assess each other's performance on the board annually. The plan would be to administer a survey of Director Performance every year and the aggregate scores would be shared with the full board."

Ron's over-confidence in the group's progress was immediately felt.

"Ron, we're volunteers for this board and we're not some paid employees that you can measure," Jerry objected.

Kevin had a nervous look on his face, as he was wondering if they had just unleashed a beast in their incoming board chair.

"Think about it, guys," Ron started. "We hold staff accountable and we need to be accountable too. Think of it as a board report card. We should welcome the feedback instead of tip-toing around hurting folk's feelings."

"As one of the people that hasn't been involved much here on the board, I can see why this is needed," Tim said. "The board needs to have something to hold directors accountable to. It becomes a way where we can have a conversation around each of our performances. Frankly, if we had this for me, I would have been out a long time ago," he concluded with a smile. The conversation seemed to shift from discontent to acceptance. Paul glanced around, unsure of whether to support the idea or to squash it. "I'm not a fan of this, I have to admit," he said with a nervous tone in his voice. "I'm not quite clear why we would need to do this, but I think it's worth a shot."

Debate continued around the merits of the idea and ultimately, the board managed to reach an agreement that they could provide input into the questions that would be used in advance. Ron directed the nominating committee to develop the annual review questions.

Deeper Controversy: Board Mentors

Ron decided that it was time to go further down the rabbit hole and stated: "As you all know, we were practically strangers pulled together and told to oversee this organization. While we all have our own strengths and weaknesses, I believe that we need to challenge our model."

Some of the directors' eyes glanced at each other in anticipation of what bombshell Ron would pitch next.

"I'd like to assign each member of the board an external mentor to help cultivate the talents and skills of each of us around this table."

Tina couldn't take it anymore: "Ron, that's preposterous. Honestly, you want us to take more time out of our schedules to meet with someone that's not even involved in the board?!"

Some of the heads nodded around the table and Ron knew he had to act quickly and decisively.

"In the world of organizational leadership, we encourage CEOs to seek mentors to help bounce ideas off of and to help build their own leadership skills. Board members are not exempt and no one teaches us what it means to be a great board director. We have to learn it through experience, but having a mentor allows us to learn from someone that has been there and done that."

"We're not talking about CEOs, Ron," Jerry was the first to weigh in, "We're talking about this company's board."

"I'm with Jerry on this one," Paul followed. "I don't think we need to waste precious time meeting with others that are not familiar with our issues."

Ron paused for a second and emphasized: "We need to explore all options that will make us the most effective board to advance Coppryx's mission. It's our duty as directors of this company. Mentoring is not a punishment but an opportunity for us to truly hone our own board leadership skills."

"I'm not opposed to this, Ron," Kevin jumped in, "but I'm worried about the level of management headaches that this may entail. But again, I'm not opposed to trying it out."

"I'm also worried about the confusion around who is going to manage these mentor relationships," Tina joined the conversation.

"We will need to work out all of the details," Ron clarified, "however, I believe we need to assign a member of the board to oversee the board mentor assignments and help take ownership of the process."

Discussion ensued further and while not Ron's perfect choice, the members agreed to pilot the concept and gave Ron the green light to identify three members of the board and to match them with mentors in order to see if the program had merit. Paul raised his hand and agreed to work with Kevin and Ron on getting the pilot off the ground.

Onwards and Upwards

With some of the major structural wins under his belt, Ron turned the floor over to Paul to discuss what was being done to help the organization adapt to its environment and to drive innovation.

Kevin surprisingly made an introductory remark: "I have to give Paul some props here. We have learned more about our clients in the past eight weeks than we have over eight years."

Paul smiled and noted how he worked with Kevin to create a series of focus groups that led them to understand more about the kind of services that they were looking for, which did not necessarily require a technology re-do of their product.

"We simply didn't know what we didn't know," Paul added. "And now that we know how to know, we're going to keep these ad hoc focus groups going throughout the year."

Paul presented some additional product changes that would allow the organization to expand some of its services and make it even more competitive. A mini-business plan was included that provided the board with an explanation of the investment costs and the ROI.

"I have to admit, I personally would like more detail around this, Paul," Jerry weighed in.

"Then join the taskforce next time, Jerry," Paul responded.

Ron could see that Paul was getting really ticked off with Jerry's prying.

"That's not a bad idea at all, Jerry," Ron commented. "How about we add you as the voice of the Finance Committee to the Product Innovation Taskforce to make sure we have cross representation. That'll also help to make sure we're all pulling on the same oar. If you agree, can we move forward on this or are there any show stoppers?" Ron asked.

"No showstoppers here," Jerry relented, "I'd like to join the group going forward."

Discussion ensued around the various product proposals but ultimately the board passed the plans. Ron also took some time to update the board on the new innovation teleconference series.

Kevin explained that they had lined up the year's speakers for the quarterly conference calls, including executives from the banking, military and transportation industries.

"Ron worked with us to develop a shortlist of topics and then we worked together to identify who would be good candidates to bring in," Kevin noted.

Jerry, always thinking from the dollars and cents side of things, without any hesitation shot his usual question: "Are we paying them?"

"Yes," Ron replied back.

Jerry smiled at the simple answer but decided to not push any further.

"Remember, innovation is not a quick fix," Ron continued. "This will take time for us to not only discuss new concepts and ideas, but the process to then test them and get them to the market will be a longer-term play here. I want to make sure we level set expectations."

With the meeting coming to a close, Ron asked the corporate board IQ taskforces to continue to meet for one more board cycle. He also noted that at the next meeting, the board would take a ground-up effort to review the strategic plan and would begin the hard work of redefining its metrics in order to include both leading and lagging indicators from the mission all the way down to strategy level.

Take-Off

Over the next 6 months, Ron and Kevin worked together to implement some of the new ideas that had been identified by the board of directors.

Ron knew that, while it was important to fill the vacant board seats as soon as possible, he had to make sure that they got it right and not rush the process. With more than half of the nine board seats available, Ron worked with Kevin to network out to others that served on boards and who had the requisite skills, as defined when they created their "ideal" board model. The new candidates also took the board character survey that indicated the kind of board director they would likely be in terms of the kind of role they may have on the board respectively. The new directors were appointed at the next meeting, which concluded the restructuring of the board composition.

The board also approved the first 180 degrees annual performance evaluation after making some small tweaks to the draft questions that were shared with the members. While it took longer than initially hoped, as several versions were drafted, Ron was happy with the finished product.

Working at the same time, Paul managed to get the board mentoring program off the ground and assigned outside mentors to each of the new board members. One of the newest members remarked to Ron what a great experience the mentoring program had been as it helped him better understand what the expectations were around the role.

On the innovation front, Ron thought he would tie together the quarterly industry expert calls with the board guest speaker program and appointed a board level "innovation chair" to the topics. The man in this new role had the responsibility to not only honcho logistics for the sessions but would also champion new ideas and ensure that the board was being challenged to think innovatively. Paul took wholeheartedly on the new role as innovation chair and truly enjoyed it.

Over this same time, a teleconference call with James Butler, COO of a ground transportation company was held. Butler hosted a session on brand differentiation with the board. Ron was surprised at how quickly the board adapted to the calls and how collegial they were. On this first call, the board spent time discussing how the challenges that they faced might also apply to Coppryx. Several ideas that arose from the call helped to influence Kevin and Ron's thinking about brand differentiation from NecroTech and other emerging competitors.

With the New Year's budget approved, Kevin's new R&D department was launched and a Chief Innovation Officer position was created to keep focus on innovation throughout the organization. Like all staff, this position reported to Kevin directly, but also had a liaison role with the board Innovation Chair (Paul) to partner on the exploration of new ideas and concepts.

Kevin and Ron worked together to create a series of focus groups that were invaluable in providing feedback to Kevin on what needed to be changed in their customer service model. Another interesting realization that Kevin made over the recent months was that in order to make a lasting positive change he needed to make internal changes at Coppryx as well. While Vanessa had served him well over the years, her inattention to detail around marketing processes had contributed to the near destruction of the organization. He had tried to coach her to be more attentive to these details but her failure to do so could no longer be ignored. As a result, Kevin replaced Vanessa with a new Vice President of Marketing.

Brand New Day

Six months had passed since the last board meeting, which now felt like an eternity. With the new directors appointed to the board, Ron spent two hours at their first board meeting discussing the seven elements of corporate board IQ with the new members.

"Our job is to check each other regularly to make sure we are not falling for any of the seven elements of corporate board IQ," Paul reminded.

Jerry decided to go biblical in response: "I am my brother's keeper."

A loud laugh fell over the board.

"We mean that it is our responsibility as a group to be honest about where we are falling down individually, or as a group and as a board," Ron interpreted.

The new directors were amazed at the level of comradery of the board and the commitment to the organization's success.

The board focused most of its session on redefining the strategic plan and set up a series of metrics and board champions to ensure that the organization was on track to achieve its goals.

Over the following months, Coppryx was able turn the tide on its customer base loss and grew sales by 25%. The new product enhancements and customer service changes made these gains possible and the new revenue was cleverly funneled back into research and development that would fuel the development of new product designs and improvements in the future.

Chapter 4:
Corporate Board Intelligence (CB-IQ)

When individuals form together as a board of directors, the group as a whole becomes larger than any individual member and becomes unique as the individual members of the board establish relationships, build roles, create norms, and execute group functions. Boards as a group tend to face similar challenges, whether they be for-profit or non-profit boards.

These commonalities are referred to as elements of Corporate Board Intelligence or CB-IQ. The surveys provided in this section allow for the individual measurement of each of the elements of corporate board IQ.

To be clear, not every organization suffers all seven of these concurrently, as it may suffer only one, a few or none at all. However, these issues are transient and these failures seem to crop up gradually. The elements that comprise CB-IQ of a board are:

1. Recruitment Stagnation: the inability of a board to fully understand what kind of skills, knowledge and personalities they need to have on the board and therefore fails to take action on those criteria set. This not only includes the selection of new board directors, but also ensures that the existing board members are held to the same standards;

2. Power Imbalance: larger boards of directors tend to push much of the work and decision making down to committees and sub-committees. While this is an effective way to divide up the workload, it can also become a choke-point for information and also render board meetings from action-oriented organizations to information-receiving only organizations. The result can be endless committee reports that dilute the board's valuable time to focus on more strategic matters;

3. Network Misalignment: boards of directors are made up of people with their own networks with other board directors. These networks play both inside and outside (more importantly) of the board room. Failure to understand these connections and how they are used leads to miscalculations in how things really get done on the board;

4. Accountability Inadequacy: The old adage "what gets measured is what gets done" is certainly true for boards of directors. Boards tend to measure surface level items that quantify operational elements of performance, but often fail to look at outcomes or measure progress to missions. Furthermore, this element encompasses the failure of boards to set specific individuals to champion and monitor progress on key strategic elements;

5. Innovation Deficiency: refers to a board of director's tendency to get caught up in existing products, services and routines and not to examine what is really working or not working, or develop new methods that can improve their operation and market position. The result is that boards tend to hold onto strategic plans that have outlived their usefulness or have become inert;

6. Environmental Maladaptation: Boards tend to handle risk and change in various manners. And while certain ideas, services and products seem good at one time, they become less and less suitable and more of a problem as time passes by. However, boards often times fall out of touch with their environments and stick with existing strategies even though market conditions have changed. Boards then fall prey to not adjusting appropriately to the market by not willing to assume enough risk to make enough changes to maintain market leadership, leading to stagnation or take on too much risk, which can deplete the organization of resources. Boards also tend to error on the "too little risk" and "too little change" side of the equation. Boards can also suffer from internal

environmental adaptation, where they also are shielded by the CEO from the internal organization and lose their optics to be able to understand what actually is happening within the organization;

7. Influence Impotence: particularly acute for mid to smaller boards, this element relates to the inability of the board of directors to have access to the right people, the right organization or the right resources. While closely tied to recruiting stagnation, this element not only looks at the issue of the lack of influence, but also whether the board exercises their connections with others for the organization's benefit. Properly structured influence allows boards to identify new opportunities that can facilitate organizational growth and connect with new talent for filling future board seats.

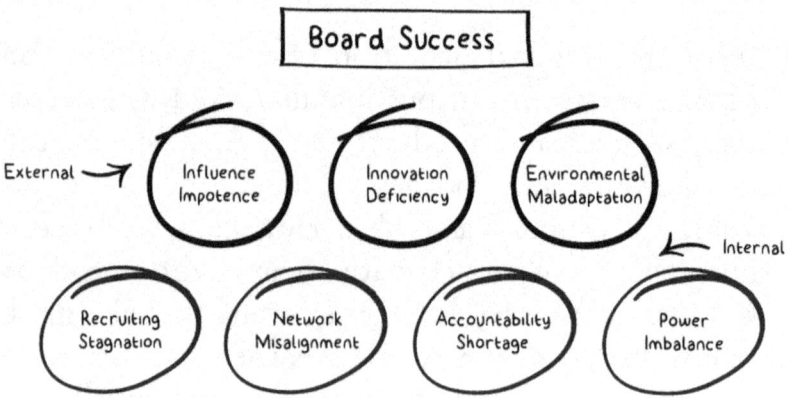

Assessing CBIQ Vulnerabilities

The survey below can be used to help evaluate your board's strengths and weaknesses regarding corporate board intelligence. The following section provides an analysis of the findings that should be reviewed with your board.

Please have each board member answer the following statements. Consider each statement from the perspective of the boards function and performance. Using a scale of 1 to 3, with 3 being the highest and 1 being the lowest, please rank how well your board performs against each of the following statements.

1. ____ The board has a good balance between looking outwards versus looking inwards
2. ____ Our board members are well connected in the industry
3. ____ Our board has the right mix of skills, experience and personalities
4. ____ Board members are held accountable for performance and conduct
5. ____ New board members are thoroughly vetted
6. ____ The board embraces innovation as strategy for growth
7. ____ The board records and reports out on outreach efforts by board members
8. ____ The board does not allow committee reports to consume too much board time
9. ____ What gets done inside the boardroom is more important then what gets done outside

10. ____ Our board is highly creative
11. ____ The COE and the board have a strong relationship
12. ____ The nominating committee does a good job of vetting candidates
13. ____ The board holds itself accountable for strategic plan success of failure
14. ____ The board utilizes their connections to advance the organization's mission
15. ____ The board monitors its own performance
16. ____ The formal board function and the informal *grapevine* are well aligned
17. ____ The board as a whole is actively involved in making critical decisions
18. ____ Our board has a good sense of threats facing our organization
19. ____ Board members are open and honest in board meetings
20. ____ The board promotes supports creative thinking and new ideas
21. ____ The right amount of power is delegated to the Executive Committee

Evaluating Scores

Now add up your scores by each of the statement categories listed below:

| Environmental Maladaptation | Statements 1, 8, 18 |
| Influence Impotence | Statements 2, 7, 14 |

Network Misalignment	Statements 9. 16. 19
Accountability Shortage	Statements 4, 13, 15
Power Imbalance	Statements 11, 17, 21
Innovation Deficiency	Statements 6, 10, 20
Recruiting Stagnation	Statements 3, 5, 12

A high score of 8 or 9 indicates a "high intelligence" in this area and that your seems to be performing appropriately in this element

A score of 6 to 7 indicates that there is room for improvement within this element

A score of 3 to 5 indicates that the board exhibited "low intelligence" in this area and steps should be strengthen to address this element

Element #1: Recruitment Stagnation

When you evaluate boards and how they begin and grow, one of the root causes of majority of the elements of corporate board IQ is the basic structure of the board. Put another way, it is the age-old problem of making sure that we have the right people in the right seats, with the right competencies, the right characters and the right commitment. When boards are initially "born", they are guided by the "bylaws", which ultimately sets the framework for the appointment of the initial board of directors. While the initial board may bring the enthusiasm and passion, invariably over time, a structure is needed to allow for the recruitment of highly effective board members.

I remember particularly one organization's board that every year during recruiting season would enter into a strong debate about the need to get more "fundraisers" or "sellers" on the board. The reasoning behind this was that the members of that particular board, while skilled in many ways, were not fundraisers, and the board needed individuals who would go out and work hard to open up new relationships that would bring in revenue. Invariably, that led the board to develop a give-or-get requirement where board members would have to agree to either give a certain amount of money, or raise it through sales or donations. This practice also led to further debate about whether only new board members should be subjected to this, or whether existing board members should as well.

All too often, these debates seem to drag on year to year without ever being resolved or criteria become watered down that they become ineffective.

Symptoms

Recruitment stagnation is particularly difficult to identify at times as it occurs over a protracted period of time. For example, one organization I worked with attracted executives to its board in its formative years, however, over time, the board of directors started appointing lower level individuals within their organizations to replace the executives, until years later there was a realization that they no longer had executive representation on the board.

Recruitment stagnation signs and symptoms present themselves in several ways, including:

1. Exceptions are made to keep board members. When a board of directors' term expires, the board tends to take action to try to change the bylaws or find other methods in order to keep the board member. The result is that newer members of the board are kept away from it in favor of existing members;
2. Higher level board members give up their seats to lower level individuals within their organizations;
3. Board attendance drops off and board members do not regularly attend the significant meetings or calls;
4. Board participation falls off and only a handful of board members are actively involved;
5. Significant chatter exists around grandfathering existing board members: when criteria are set for recruiting new members, existing Board members grandfather themselves in, in order to avoid having the same responsibilities;
6. Backroom conversations exist about having the "wrong kind" of board members. When not in the board room, discontent builds among some board members that the board either has the long "level" or wrong "skills" of Board members;

7. Decreased interest in outside candidates to run for the board because they think it's a "lock" for existing members: prospective candidates will tell the CEO or other members of the board that they are not bothering to run because they just re-elect the same individuals.

Prevention & Treatment Strategies

The answer ultimately is that the best board of directors realize they are running something akin to the NFL Combine, where they are trying to recruit the best talent that they can acquire. Each season is an opportunity to improve the position of the team (or in this case the board of directors). Below are some prevention and treatment strategies:

Develop an Ideal Board Composition State

You would be surprised at how often boards of directors recruit without any concept of what kind of players they need. I suggest engaging your board in a discussion on what is the ideal board state, taking out the current directors. Creating a list of desired set of competencies first is a must (e.g finance, HR, IT, Government Relations, Sales, Investments, Mergers, Legal, etc.). Rank these and weight them by asking what percentage of the board should have these skills. The next step is to properly evaluate character types of your existing directors and develop a composite view of what percentage you should have of each character type (e.g. Marine,

Backgrounder, etc.). Clearly, you won't and practically could not find the same group of people with the exact same skills, experience and characters.

Rank Existing Board Directors against the Ideal State

Once you have completed the ideal matrix, before you start recruiting, evaluate the board of directors as it currently stands around how they fit. You may be surprised. For example, if you said that you needed a heavy split of sales oriented individuals on the board and you find that you are heavy on Finance skills with existing board members, you may need to make adjustments to existing board seats. One note of caution is to avoid "fitting the square peg in the round hole." Put another way, avoid watering down your criteria set, in order to avoid having to deal with the uncomfortable situation where a director may not fit the criteria.

Understand Your Board Character Types

Admittedly, I have found personalities are much harder to evaluate in a recruiting matrix, but have also realized over years of observing boards of directors that individuals do indeed tend to fall into buckets. I have provided a list of these personality types below with observable characteristics and urge all organizations to get a full understanding of how many directors fall into these categories. A full survey is available in the next section that you can use to help identify the various types of personalities of board members:

a) **Whisperer:** this personality type is a master of informal networks and is very aware of who talks to who on the board of directors and leverage back channel communications to share their own desires or concerns. Individuals with this personality type are less likely to openly communicate their feelings within the board room itself and will defer to stronger personalities on the board.

b) **Saber Rattler:** these individuals are typically the first ones in the board room to say something negative, or to attack an idea or concept. They typically are outwardly proud of this personality attribute. They do not fear confrontation and in fact, thrive on it. They tend to have these traits in their primary workplace and even in their personal relationships. They are less likely to participate in informal networks or would discount information from the informal network in favor of their own viewpoint on a specific matter.

c) **Soothsayer (aka Futurist):** this personality type is rarer than the others and this kind of individuals usually enjoy looking at future alternative states and engaging in dialogue around big concepts, ideas and thoughts of what "can be done". These individuals are incredibly useful in strategic planning exercises and helping to develop new innovative ideas and concepts. They are comfortable playing with complex ideas that are untested and unconventional. However, one negative element of this personality type is that they are easily bored by mundane issues and do not necessarily want to be bothered with execution level details or any kind of boring tasks that boards engage in.

d) **Influencer:** these individuals are often sought after by boards of directors, as they tend to be highly outward, confident and well-spoken people that are well connected within their given industry. They are not afraid of rejection and typically maintain vast contacts, which they are not afraid to use in order to advance their specific cause or goals. Influencers are highly outspoken and typically very friendly. They are socially very engaged in board functions and may participate eagerly in outward facing issues that boards face. They are most sought after, as these individuals are likely to have contacts that can open up new business opportunities for the boards that they serve on.

e) **Backgrounder:** not all members of a particular board are interested in being active participants. In fact, for some boards over 50% of its members may fall into this category. This type of board director mainly attends meetings, but is otherwise absent from the work of the board. They are generally well-meaning individuals that tend to agree with the more vocal majority of the board. They tend to not take on activities outside of the meetings, but may participate in informal networks socially (particularly around board meetings). They are "backgrounders", because they simply exist in the background and do not actively engage.

f) **Parliamentarian:** every congress needs a parliamentarian. These are typically outspoken individuals that place an extraordinary focus on rules of order and policies and procedures. However, this outspokenness is often taken to an extreme, as the individual is willing to spend an inordinate amount of time of board meeting time to address such issues and may use the rules focus to derail other progress. These individuals tend to be very hands-on and involved in the matters of board operations and can be useful to ensure that their established protocols are thoroughly followed. However, they can be quite intractable at times and find it difficult to entertain new concepts or ideas that may challenge the status quo.

g) **Saboteur:** this is a very rare type of board director but can occasionally pop up in boards. These individuals are not well-wishers to the organization for either personal or business reasons. They have certain personal agendas that just may not mesh or be in the best interest of the boards that they serve on. These individuals may or may not appear as being "hostile" in a meeting, but will use their formal and informal powers to slow down or derail board action that they see as detrimental to their own interest. This is the most dangerous personality type of board director and is more likely to occur when boards allow organizations with competing interests to serve on the board.

h) **Financier:** while this is a skill and a role on the board (treasurer), this is also a personality type. Very similar to the Parliamentarian, the Financier is highly focused on the financial reporting and management of the organization. They are typically detailed individuals that enjoy being mired in the financial statements and audit reports. Since most board directors do not enjoy this level of detail, they are highly deferred to by other members of the board on financial matters. These individuals also tend to be very hands-on and involved in matters of board operations but can be very useful in evaluating the costs of new initiatives and strategic plans.

i) **Marine:** this personality type loves to be on the "tip of the spear" of new initiatives. Where other personality types (e.g. Parliamentarian) are content with helping to manage the operational aspects of the board, the Marine loves the idea of new concepts (like the Soothsayer), but is the front line solider that is tapped to take an idea and can be counted upon to execute it. Marines are rarer than other board types but are extremely useful in helping to enact bold new ideas and strategies. Marines do tend to get bored easily like Soothsayers, as they need to be out wrestling with a new idea and bringing action to bear.

Assessing Board Character Type

The following survey can be used to help evaluate each board member with a primary and secondary board character. The primary board character type means that a board member is likely to display this type of behavior regularly. A secondary board character type means that the board member may not always display this behavior tendency, but will do so occasionally. The following section provides an analysis of the findings that should be reviewed with your board.

Please have each board member answer the following statements. Quickly answer each question, without reflecting too much on the statement. Using a scale of 1 to 3, with 3 being the highest, meaning this statement describes you; 2 meaning that this may occasionally describe you or 1 being the lowest, which means this statement does not describe you at all.

1. _____ Our business plans need more financial rigor
2. _____ I find it difficult to find time to fully engage in the board of the work
3. _____ I believe rules, order, policies and procedures must always be followed
4. _____ I find it hard to attend board meetings
5. _____ I consider myself a visionary
6. _____ I prefer listening over speaking in formal meetings
7. _____ I work outside of the board room to get agreement

8. ____ I tend attack new ideas or concepts in order to get more information
9. ____ I am probably one of the most vocal members of the board
10. ____ I believe we need more emphasis on financial analysis of our initiatives
11. ____ I feel uncomfortable in communicating openly at board meetings
12. ____ I leverage back channel communications to share my desires or concerns
13. ____ I give adequate time to my board obligations
14. ____ I tend to agree with the general consensus of the board
15. ____ I am skeptical until proven otherwise
16. ____ My personal interest and the boards interest are not well aligned
17. ____ I believe I am highly focused on financial reports and our financial discipline
18. ____ I am comfortable playing with complex ideas that are untested and unconventional
19. ____ Others probably perceive me as aggressive or confrontational
20. ____ I never allow rules and procedures to be broken at our meetings
21. ____ I enjoy the details of financial statements and audit reports
22. ____ I'm willing to use my influence to slow board actions I disagree with
23. ____ I believe the board needs to do a better job of financial management

24. ____ My board involvement is good for my own career or business interest
25. ____ I like to meet with other board members outside of the scheduled board activites
26. ____ I tend to be the realist in the board room
27. ____ I'm willing to stop debate if I believe the rules of order are not being followed
28. ____ Others may feel that I appear hostile in board meetings
29. ____ I get frustrated whenever established protocols are not followed appropriately
30. ____ Others perceive me as actively involved in the board
31. ____ Others most likely perceive me as a *people person*
32. ____ The possibilities that our organization can achieve are endless
33. ____ I tend to get bored by mundane issues
34. ____ I am one of the hardest working people on this board
35. ____ I enjoy exploring new ideas and concepts
36. ____ I consider myself a strong networker
37. ____ Sometimes my own agenda does not mesh with the board's
38. ____ I believe I am effective at getting what I want done behind the scenes
39. ____ Others on the board probably consider my involvement to be quite passive
40. ____ I consider myself highly persuasive on the board
41. ____ I'm highly involved in board activities

42. ____ I believe confrontation should be avoided at board meetings
43. ____ I tend to like to watch things unfold
44. ____ I enjoy struggling with new and complex ideas
45. ____ I enjoy finding ways to connect with people
46. ____ Sometimes people's feelings have to get hurt at board meetings

Evaluating Scores

Now add up your scores by each of the statement categories listed below:

Financier	Statements 1, 10, 17, 21, 23
Backgrounder	Statements 2, 4, 14, 25, 43
Whisperer	Statements 38, 42, 12, 11, 6
Parliamentarian	Statements 3, 9, 20, 29, 27
Soothsayer	Statements 5, 18, 32, 33, 44
Influencer	Statements 31. 36. 40, 7, 45
Marine	Statements 34, 39, 41, 13, 20
Saber Rattler	Statements 8, 15, 19, 26, 46
Saboteur	Statements 16, 22, 24, 28, 37

A high score of 11 or higher indicates your dominate board character style.

A score of 6 to 10 indicates your secondary board character style.

A score of 1 to 5 indicates that you rarely exhibits these character styles.

If multiple character types are ranking highly, sort the character styles from highest to lowest. The highest scored will be your primary and secondary board character styles.

Enforce the Ideal State on New & Current Directors

It goes without saying that once the ideal state matrix is developed, it must be enforced for new directors. However, more importantly, you must rank existing board members to this and then enforce whether they continue to fit the board profile as defined. It's imperative that the existing board be evaluated on a regular basis in order to determine an ongoing fit. Some boards are not willing to do this because they fear the conflict from having to have a conversation with the individuals that may not fit. Great boards realize that they do not hold seats for life, rather their allegiance advances the mission of the organization. This can and will lead to difficult conversations that board chairs must have with the board of directors around whether some board members should stay or move off the board. We suggest that a group of three individuals be identified to help hold difficult conversations.

In some cases, where the shift is too dramatic, I have seen some organizations develop a timeline where they ask a certain number of members off the board over a two- or three-year period as they recruit the desired candidates. In only one case that I have ever seen in my career, a full board of directors voted themselves out in favor of an entirely new board. It took a lot of nerve and courage for the board to do that, but it did lead them to a quick-fix in changing the board composition. A word of caution - if some existing directors need to be replaced, make sure that it is not done over such a long time frame that it impacts new directors. There is nothing worse than cases when new directors are given one set of commitments and then upon meeting the existing directors, they learn that they are not held to the same standard.

Empower the Nominating Committee

In some cases, nominating committees can be "toothless dogs", particularly in organizations where there is a larger election process (e.g. membership based organizations). However, even in such environments, nominating committee must have the responsibility to reject candidates for not meeting the board's desired needs matrix. The ideal state matrix is the true north for nominating committee. It is recommended that nominating committees be given the authority to reject candidates for not meeting the ideal state matrix prior to being passed to the board for approval.

Element #2: Network Misalignment

I remember as a young executive watching how things supposedly "got done" versus how they actually got done. Board meetings tend to look like kabuki theatre. There's a lot of make-up, on-stage acting and structure at an actual board meeting. In 2005, I completed my doctoral dissertation that evaluated how formal and informal networks interacted within an organization to advance its learning. Through my research, I found that every organization has these two faces, and boards of directors are not exception.

As a board leader or CEO, one critical element to understand is that there is a vast system of networks of individuals that lay underneath the board. We can therefore conceive of the board of directors into two different worlds - one that is formal and palpable (e.g. the board meetings and official roles) and one that is informal, based on relationships and information exchanges outside of the formal structure.

In my own doctoral research, I found eight primary types of networks and exchanges that play out, including: gossip, task orientation, conflict, trust, advice, influence, personal information and support.

Board members engage in various forms of types of communication whether it's at the board meeting in-person, or outside of the board room (which is actually more common). These information networks are critically important to the function of an organization and to the board, as they serve as a safe environment for the organization to address difficult conversations.

The formal board structure and informal board networks maintain a tumultuous, yet symbiotic relationship within the collective learning process. Formal board meetings and structures tend to keep a focus on task-oriented knowledge and are in place to maintain system cohesion. They are the glue that keeps the organization focused on achieving goals.

The informal organization serves as a pressure valve for the formal organization, dealing with conflict without disrupting the functioning of the formal organization.

Symptoms

Clearly, not all informal networks are bad and in fact, they are an important process for boards to get to agreement, or to deal with dissent. However, network misalignment can negatively impact board performance. Similar to the way how the CIA looks for terrorists to start communicating with each other about a potential attack, so can boards spot possible network misalignment as well. The informal network is what we call "porous", like a sponge, and just like a sponge, it leaks…a lot. The reason is that people love gossip and they're terrible at keeping secrets.

When these networks are misaligned, chaos can reign under the deck of the ship, which reverberates through the board meetings themselves. For example, if there is a controversial issue that is not being dealt with at the board meeting, it is almost a guarantee that it will be dealt with informally. Every CEO knows this intuitively, namely that most of the work of the board is done outside of the board room. As a CEO myself, I can remember "counting votes" like it was election night before going into the board room with a controversial vote, or a particularly difficult agenda item. The ability to understand those networks and how they align is crucial to a successful board.

Below are some key symptoms of network misalignment:

1. Excessive network chatter with many side conversations, or you are hearing about these from other people;
2. Patterns of negative comments made in the informal networks appears at the formal board meetings (e.g. specific complaints);
3. Specific groups of directors tend to consistently meet outside of the board meetings and tend to be more negative than other members at the meeting;
4. Certain directors do not engage with the core group socially or tend to isolate themselves;
5. Certain sets of directors tend to clump together on negative decisions;
6. Certain sets of directors are quiet on the board and defer to individuals that are willing to express negativity.

Prevention & Treatment Strategies

Preventing misalignment is much easier to solve for them than the actual treatment. When misalignment occurs, there is often an environment of mistrust that has created a great need of the informal network to become more active. Below are some key strategies to ensure network alignment:

1. Eliminate directors that may not fit. Eliminating specific directors that may contribute to ongoing disputes or who do not fit the ideal state (under recruiting stagnation) is one method that allows boards to disrupt the imbalance by eliminating a "ringleader";
2. Facilitating more social engagements and ties together actually can reverse the problem of misalignment and ensure that the formal organization of the board is building strong ties. This dilutes the effects of the limited strong ties that may have been developed behind the scenes (informally);
3. Place Term Limits on directors. The longer that ties are in place, the more they bind. While this can be a good thing, it can be a bad one as well, as the long established relationships can bind directors from seeing new opportunities and can lead to network misalignment that is hard to displace. Term limits force the issue by breaking the age-old ties that bind the board together formally;

4. Confront complexity head-on: network misalignment thrives when the board faces complex problems and crises (e.g. revenue drops, executive turnover, lawsuits, etc.). Creating opportunities for organizations to deal with crises together as a unit at the board meetings or through special calls helps to weaken chances for network misalignment;
5. Intentional Insertion of individuals who are willing to infiltrate the network in order to provide information to the formal network (e.g. board chair), or to inject information intended to reduce the tension in the informal network.

Element #3: Power Imbalance

With larger boards particularly, extensive committee, sub-committee or taskforce infrastructure is put in place in order to break up the workload and to help organize efforts of board work. These committees are often given a distinct set of functions and are asked to provide recommendations back to a full board of directors. Committees are extremely important, as they allow the board to advance work that would not be possible in the course of a board meeting.

Power imbalance happens when committees either get too much "power" or do so much work that they render the work of the board mute. For example, in one organization they formed a strategic planning committee whose job was to develop a new strategic plan for the board of directors to consider. The committee went off diligently about its work with a subset of the board. When the suggested revisions came back to the board of directors for review, a number of the directors that had not been on the strategic planning committee became extremely agitated, as they felt like they had been denied the opportunity to weigh in on the strategic plan. Ultimately, the board chair dissolved the strategic planning committee and moved the strategic plan creation process to a "committee of the whole board". This actually led to an elongated strategic planning process that was extremely cumbersome and difficult to navigate given the sheer volume of board members.

Power imbalance happens when either too much or too little power is delegated down to board committees, sub-committees or taskforces.

Symptoms

Of all of the sins, Power Imbalance is relatively easy to spot and manifests itself in three manners:

1. Side-ways: The Executive Committee makes decisions and the full board feels like they have no input;
2. Bottom-up: The board committees do most of the work and provide reports back to the full board of directors. The result is that the full board feels like they are there to rubber stamp decisions made by committees;

3. Top-down: The board does all of the work and does not delegate down to committees or delegates. The result is that committees feel like they do not make a difference and are not engaged.

Prevention & Treatment Strategies

Treatment and correction of this element are relatively easy as well compared to the other elements:

1. Evaluate the opinions of other directors through an annual survey to determine if they feel the balance of power is correct, or to determine if there is disenfranchisement;
2. Consciously design committee structures to ensure appropriate power is delegated. Many boards tend to make committees without evaluating how they will change the power dynamics. Make an effort to understand who has authority and how much authority will be granted to each committee;
3. Ensure that each committee's chair or liaison is actively reporting and involved at the full board level;
4. Create opportunities for committees to engage boards of directors with key questions and provide frequent opportunities for input;
5. Avoid using the executive committee as a substitute for the full board of directors or using the executive committee to avoid dealing with an unwieldy board structure;

6. Ensure that the board is properly sized. Many boards will use committees as a way to get around dealing with size issues. Deal with the size issue head-on. It is understood that not all boards are small or should be small, but this should be consciously addressed.

Element #4: Accountability Inadequacy

Board leadership typically focuses on the legal and fiduciary nature of their responsibilities when they think of accountability. However, while important, there is much more to accountability. Often times, boards may think about CEO performance plans and compensation, which again is critical, but is only a part of this element.

Often there is a pre-occupation with the measurement of the most visible parts of the organization only and those measurements are usually focused on lagging measures, meaning that the event has passed for the measurement to be measured. This ultimately means that organizations are more likely to miss critical events because they are measuring the wrong thing, or the event has already passed by the time they become aware of it.

A second part of this element is the failure of boards is the over-delegation of responsibility. Under this scenario, boards do not hold themselves accountable for strategic plan success and place full accountability on the CEO and the executive team to execute. Short of receiving measurement updates at board meetings, the plan is completely delegated. This common decision distances the board of directors from the strategic plan and unknowingly weakens the partnership between the board and staff to ultimately ensure plan execution and success.

Symptoms

The following symptoms of the Accountability Inadequacy are evident through:

1. Over-delegation of performance metrics to executive staff without proper leading and lagging indicators that truly measure success;
2. No metrics related to an organization's vision, mission or key goals;
3. Limited amount of leading indicators, which limits the ability of the board to see what can be expected in the future;
4. Too many metrics - Boards are unable to discern if goals are being directionally achieved or not, due to the sheer volume of metrics reported;
5. Over-occupation with metrics - in some cases, it may not be the quantity of metrics but the amount of board time spent. There is a balance that must be achieved between too much and too little;
6. No board directors are assigned as champions for specific goals. This leads to a large disconnect between staff and the board on strategic plan success;

7. No board accountability for strategic plan failure. No measurement exist of each board member's contribution to the strategic plan.

Prevention & Treatment Strategies

As boards of directors look to establish effective strategies around accountability and performance measurements, I encourage a number of steps they should take on to ensure the optimal balance:

1. Audit existing outcomes to determine what they are measuring or not measuring. We suggest that boards form an ad hoc performance team in order to evaluate key metrics used by both the board of directors and by executive staff. This will foster a mutual understanding of what is "paid attention to" and helps to set a baseline to work from to determine if these outcomes are effective.

   Below is an example of an exercise I use in order to evaluate my client's measurement:

   Please check each existing measurement in a column. Determine what "level" of measurement is currently in place, whether the measurement is leading or lagging, and who is currently using the metric (board or CEO, or both). An example below demonstrates:

   a. Impact measures
      i. Vision and Mission
   b. Activity measures (Strategy)

    i. Services launched
    ii. Customer satisfaction
  c. Capacity Measures (Tactical)
    i. Press mentions
    ii. Number of widgets sold
    iii. Attendees at a conference

2. Brainstorm with a number of directors, staff and perhaps outside experts to evaluate what could be possibly leading and lagging metrics at all three levels. Rank the importance of these metrics and create a new column on the timing that the metrics should be evaluated;
3. Very simply - ask existing directors if they feel informed appropriately about performance; do they have a good balance between leading and lagging indicators; and do they feel they have personal ownership over the achievement of goals;
4. Evaluate the talents of each director and assign a director for each goal or strategy. These champions' job is to not only monitor between board meetings progress, but to also actively champion the cause, to help break down barriers and to assist the CEO in communicating board directors (both informing and gathering feedback);
5. Great boards hold themselves accountable. Holding an annual 180 degree performance review of the board's performance against the strategic plan's success of failure creates important feedback for the directors individually and as a group. Additionally, it builds a natural inflection point that boards can use to discuss how the board can improve their strategic roles.

Element #5: Innovation Deficiency

Innovation deficiency is difficult often times for boards to assess themselves, as they are the proverbial "mice on the wheel" in that they are trapped in the existing system and unable to see where or how they are deficient.

Innovation deficiency occurs when organizations tend to get comfortable in their local environments and tend to not scan their environments for new ideas. It's similar to putting a cast on an arm and losing muscle strength over time since the muscle is not used.

Innovation deficiency is often only seen when it is too late, or when organizations start to suffer from performance problems (e.g. drops in revenue). Boards tend to believe that if they are successful, then they will continue to be successful or delegate innovation to the organization's staff leadership as something they need to address.

Symptoms

There are a number of warning lights that go off that organizations should be on the look-out for, including:

1. Some organizations simply do not critically evaluate their product and service portfolio and allow them to stagnate. Organizations that experience this tend to only start thinking about product and service stagnation after they see a decline in market share;

2. Many boards tend to either not measure critical success at all, or confuse measuring performance as a surrogate for innovation. New innovation must be monitored and boards of directors need to create metrics that allow them to keep track of how innovation is being implemented;
3. Often times, innovators come in and disrupt the market around existing places (think Netflix versus BlockBuster). New entrants should send signals to the board of directors that it's time to evaluate whether the strategies remain germane or need to be modified;
4. If board meetings do not talk about new ideas or concepts, there should be concern regarding limited experimentation. Boards tend to frown on experimentation because it's messy, it costs money and there is no guaranteed outcome. Boards must build a culture of "play" that allows them in addition to the staffed organization to try out new ideas and to experiment;
5. The board does not know what the research and development (R&D) budget is or the R&D budget is insufficient. Some organizations do not understand how much they have allocated for research and development or too little is dedicated. Both of these are warning signs that innovation deficiency is not far behind.

Prevention & Treatment Strategies

Prevention and treatment focus on opening up the board to allow themselves the ability to be innovative. These strategies include:

1. Appointment of an innovation chair in order to keep focus on the topic of innovation. This also allows innovation to maintain a spot on the agenda as an ongoing focus for the board;
2. Create a direct liaison role between the board innovation chair and an organization Chief Innovation Officer (if the position exists) to foster closer board to staff alignment, and to accelerate identification and testing of new ideas;
3. Develop a guest speaker program through occasional teleconferences and for board meetings that pick a specific topic and include conversation with the speaker to bounce ideas off of;
4. Build in cross-industry expertise, whether through welcoming them as speakers or appointing them as board directors. It enables the board to think about problems differently through the added experience from other industries;
5. Appoint special advisory boards of customers, future customers or industry experts to provide an ongoing focus on innovation and to help develop new ideas or challenge existing ones held by the board or management;
6. Set aside time at each board meeting to play. Boards need to build in slack time to consider new ideas, to

discuss outside ideas and to generally explore uncomfortable topics in order to develop new innovation. While innovation does and can occur within the staffed organization, boards can be a powerful force in facilitating new innovation.

Element #6: Environmental Maladaptation

Environmental maladaptation is a critical condition that can tear apart organizations at the seams by cementing them in their past. I would imagine at some point in time, the board of directors at Kodak must have looked back on their leadership and thought they should have seen the rise of the digital camera coming.

However, all organizations have the potential to fail in the same way. In a particular organization I observed, it was evident that they were seeing their market share slowly being chipped away by other competitors. The CEO at the time worked with the board to develop a strategic plan that was quite bold and dramatic. However, the plan ultimately was watered down and those things that were considered "riskier" were prioritized so low that what would have been an aggressive plan ended up looking quite marginal. The result was the organization never made change because they would not assume the level of risk needed to make the change.

Adaptation is a two-way street. It is an organization's ability to sense changes (see the changes) and then secondly, to be bold enough to take the risks and change itself.

Additionally, some boards may be environmentally maladapted internally as well, without having an adequate understanding of the operations of the organizations, or being too insulated by the CEO from the organization that they lose perspective of reality.

Symptoms

Like many issues that boards face on a regular basis, this particular condition typically has a gradual onset and is the culmination of a series of decisions, rather than just one single decision. Organizations should be on the lookout for the following symptoms:

1. Strategic plans in these organizations typically suffer from dust bunnies sitting on the strategic plans. Plans are typically executed and then not evaluated on a regular basis, nor do they have metrics to determine success of the strategic plans;
2. Boards spend limited time looking outward. While internal oversight is a part of the board, it's the external facing part of the board that often gets ignored;
3. Similar to the aforementioned symptom, we find that boards suffering from this element tend to fill their agendas with committee reports and internal functions, and do not externally engage their great environment;

4. Boards can become institutionalized over time and find it difficult to break from history. Being stuck in "how we did it" tends to freeze boards from being able to adapt to their larger environments;
5. Similar to the same sign in innovation deficiency, if board meetings do not talk about new ideas or concepts, there should be concern regarding limited experimentation. Boards trend to frown on experimentation because it's messy. It costs money and there is no guaranteed outcome.

Prevention & Treatment Strategies

Prevention and treatment are very similar to those of innovation deficiency and focus on giving the board opportunities to scan their environment and to effectively learn. These strategies include:

1. Develop a guest speaker program through occasional teleconferences and for board meetings that pick a specific topic and include conversation with the speaker to bounce ideas off of;
2. Build in cross-industry expertise, whether through welcoming them as speakers or appointing them as board directors, it allows the board access to think about problems differently through the added experience from other industries;
3. Appoint special advisory boards of customers, future customers or industry experts in order to provide an ongoing focus on innovation, and to

help develop new or challenge existing ideas held by the board or management;
4. Set aside time at each board meeting to consider new ideas, products or services;
5. Develop an advisory council that provides input to the board of directors on new ideas and concepts.

Element #7: Influence Impotence

A critical exterior factor and one of the key reasons for boards existence, is their ability to open up an organization to new ideas and markets that they may not have had access to otherwise. Some refer to this as "social capital", or the social relationships that one has in the greater community and their ability to leverage those social connections. Influence and access go together hand-in-hand, as directors are often selected for their contacts and willingness to use those contacts to advance the organizations for which they serve.

Influence importance occurs when the existing directors neither have the skills or contacts to fulfill this role, nor do not take an active role in using their external networks to improve the position of the board.

Often times, this element can be closely associated to recruitment stagnation, as mentioned earlier in this book. Boards through their nominating processes have opportunities to ensure that the individuals that they have onboard contain the required external networking skills. However, boards tend to evolve over time, both in their funding and who they may have access to in their recruiting pool of candidates. For example, a well to do for-profit organization that offers paid board positions will have a much easier time to locate talent compared to a local non-profit charity that have started recently.

Symptoms

There are a number of signs that boards may see over time that indicate a problem here. It is important to remember that there are two parts of this element- the lack of access and the unwillingness to use influence on behalf of the organization. Organizations should be on the lookout for the following symptoms:

1. The board spends time "complaining" about the lack of individuals without the right connections or the lack of "executive" level experience on the board;
2. Informal chatter about the board composition or how the board lacks the correct type of members;
3. Issues to improve board composition either at the nominating committee level of board directors go nowhere, but never seem to completely go away;
4. Discussion focuses on how to raise the bar for board commitments for new board directors;
5. Existing board directors do not provide any sales connections, introductions, or donations;
6. Board members will discuss how they give their time and talent but are not comfortable giving money or selling.

Prevention & Treatment Strategies

1. Implement an annual board director performance review for evaluating how directors contribute to new sales leads, introduction or made a donation. This will create accountability for each director and shines a light on those that may also have connections but are not using them to benefit the organization;
2. Evaluate board directors against the ideal board state defined in the recruitment stagnation section. If those that were brought in to fill such roles are not able or willing to use their influence, consider their removal from the board of directors;
3. Create opportunities for directors to build and leverage social connections on behalf of the organization through organized dinners or events with stakeholders. Repeated exposure to connections builds greater likeliness that a connection will be built or exploited for the benefit of the organization;
4. Use competitions and recognition for board directors that leverage their influence on behalf of the organization. As human beings, we crave social contact and also seek praise for our actions. Using recognition efforts in front of board peers or competitions helps to fulfill those basic needs and also injects fun into the influence process;
5. Spend time focused on influence. At board meetings, discuss certain problems that would be resolved with director connections and influence.

Come up with a plan to engage those connections and assign staff to follow-up with the directors to ensure that those assigned connections are completed;

6. Create a rallying cry. As humans, we tend to rise above when confronted with an issue (e.g. war, economic crisis, etc.). Board members will engage more around influence if they can see a benefit to the group and that their personal involvement is crucial to the success of the project.

Where's Leadership

There has been much written in the business world landscape about whether leadership makes a difference or not in organizations, governments and teams. My experience shows that a good leader certainly can't hurt a board of directors, but a bad leader certainly can. One former board chair, quoting Alexander the Great, used to tell me: "I'd rather have an army of sheep led by a lion than an army of lions led by a sheep."

And while I do not discount the fact that poor leadership would more likely lead to poor outcomes, I've also seen strong boards survive and thrive through poor leadership. Boards of directors therefore cannot be conceived of as only the chair of the board or the elected officers. Power is more distributed among board directors given that boards tend to attract the same levels of individuals. Those individuals who exhibit the greatest confidence or visible dedication tend to rise in the ranks of elected positions.

While there are methods to evaluate and recruit for certain leadership attributes, I believe that the innovation capacity and the risk and adaptation tolerances of the board as a whole are more important.

Another point worth making regarding leadership is that of the CEO. Some may believe that Kevin was too weak and passive as a CEO in managing the board, and you would be correct. I crafted the CEO that way in order to put a bright light on the board's function. CEOs play an incredibly important part of highly performing boards. However, in some cases, CEO can "over lead", where boards acquiesce to the CEO and rubber stamp most decisions.

Summary

Great boards don't just happen, they require deliberate action, active reflection and the willingness to make difficult changes. Leading boards is different than leading organizations. They have no supervisors and all directors are equal. However, these boards have the ability to unlock incredible potential for the organizations in which they are entrusted to lead. All too often, boards lack the courage to make changes necessary.

These 7 elements of Corporate Board Intelligence (CB-IQ) of innovation deficiency, environmental maladaptation, recruitment stagnation, network misalignment, accountability inadequacy, and influence impotence happen to almost every board at some point in time in their lifetime. As a board member or CEO, your job is to be ever vigilant for these elements of CB-IQ and to help prevent against them or atone for them quickly when they are discovered before they erode organizational performance.

Dedication

I dedicate this book to my incredible family, who are my inspiration, my joy and my love.

To my incredible wife, Sandhya, I cannot thank you enough. Your encouragement is the primary reason why this book ever got off the ground. Your love has given me the confidence that I can truly achieve anything I aspire to. Thank you for your inspiration, your everlasting love, and your friendship. As I said in our vows almost 10 years ago; I love with you beyond all measure, beyond all time, and beyond all words.

To my children, Rohin, Talin and Aeowyn, thank you for allowing me to learn more from you than I can ever teach you in this world. I'm truly blessed with the honor of being your father.

I also dedicate this book to my beloved mom and dad. I'm grateful for your constant love and support throughout my life, for helping me reinforce my faith and encouraging me in my endless pursuit of knowledge.

www.ingramcontent.com/pod-product-compliance
Lightning Source LLC
Chambersburg PA
CBHW070319190526
45169CB00005B/1669